Don't Fear the Reaper: 250 Anecdotes

David Bruce

Published by David Bruce, 2022.

DON'T FEAR THE REAPER: 250 ANECDOTES

First edition. September 9, 2022.

ISBN: 979-8215005538

Written by David Bruce.

Table of Contents

Dedication

Dedicated to Carl Eugene Bruce and Josephine Saturday Bruce

My father, Carl Eugene Bruce, died on 24 October 2013. He used to work for Ohio Power, and at one time, his job was to shut off the electricity of people who had not paid their bills. He sometimes would find a home with an impoverished mother and some children. Instead of shutting off their electricity, he would tell the mother that she needed to pay her bill or soon her electricity would be shut off. He would write on a form that no one was home when he stopped by because if no one was home he did not have to shut off their electricity.

The best good deed that anyone ever did for my father occurred after a storm that knocked down many power lines. He and other linemen worked long hours and got wet and cold. Their feet were freezing because water got into their boots and soaked their socks. Fortunately, a kind woman gave my father and the other linemen dry socks to wear.

My mother, Josephine Saturday Bruce, died on 14 June 2003. She used to work at a store that sold clothing. One day, an impoverished mother with a baby clothed in rags walked into the store and started shoplifting in an interesting way: The mother took the rags off her baby and dressed the infant in new clothing. My mother knew that this mother could not afford to buy the clothing, but she helped the mother dress her baby and then she watched as the mother walked out of the store without paying.

***

The doing of good deeds is important. As a free person, you can choose to live your life as a good person or as a bad person. To be a good person, do good deeds. To be a bad person, do bad deeds. If you do good deeds, you will become good. If you do bad deeds, you will become bad. To become the person you want to be, act as if you already are that kind of person. Each of us chooses what kind of person we will become. To become a good person, do the things a good person does. To become a bad person, do the things a bad person does. The opportunity to take action to become the kind of person you want to be is yours.

Human beings have free will. According to the Babylonian Niddah 16b, whenever a baby is to be conceived, the Lailah (angel in charge of contraception) takes the drop of semen that will result in the conception and asks God, "Sovereign of the Universe, what is going to be the fate of this drop? Will it develop into a robust or into a weak person? An intelligent or a stupid person? A wealthy or a poor person?" The Lailah asks all these questions, but it does not ask, "Will it develop into a righteous or a wicked person?" The answer to that question lies in the decisions to be freely made by the human being that is the result of the conception.

A Buddhist monk visiting a class wrote this on the chalkboard: "EVERYONE WANTS TO SAVE THE WORLD, BUT NO ONE WANTS TO HELP MOM DO THE DISHES." The students laughed, but the monk then said, "Statistically, it's highly unlikely that any of you will ever have the opportunity to run into a burning orphanage and rescue an infant. But, in the smallest gesture of kindness — a warm smile, holding the door for the person behind you, shoveling the driveway of the elderly person next door — you have committed an act of immeasurable profundity, because to each of us, our life is our universe."

In her book titled *I Have Chosen to Stay and Fight*, comedian Margaret Cho writes, "I believe that we get complimentary snack-size portions of the afterlife, and we all receive them in a different way." For Ms. Cho, many of her snack-size portions of the afterlife come in hip hop music. Other people get different snack-size portions of the afterlife, and we all must be on the lookout for them when they come our way. And perhaps doing good deeds and experiencing good deeds are snack-size portions of the afterlife.

The Zen master Gisan was taking a bath. The water was too hot, so he asked a student to add some cold water to the bath. The student brought a bucket of cold water, added some cold water to the bath, and then threw the rest of the water on a rocky path. Gisan scolded the student: "Everything can be used. Why did you waste the rest of the water by pouring it on the path? There are some plants nearby which could have used the water. What right do you have to waste even a drop of water?" The student became enlightened and changed his name to Tekisui, which means "Drop of Water."

Front Cover Photograph for *Don't Fear the Reaper: 250 Anecdotes*:
https://pixabay.com/photos/dead-party-halloween-1022163/

***

This is a short, quick, and easy read.

Anecdotes are usually short humorous stories. Sometimes they are thought-provoking or informative, not amusing.

***

Educate Yourself
Read Like A Wolf Eats
Be Excellent to Each Other
Books Then, Books Now, Books Forever

***

Do you know a language other than English? If you do, I give you permission to translate this book, copyright your translation, publish or self-publish it, and keep all the royalties for yourself. (Do give me credit, of course, for the original book.)

Dedicated with Respect to
the Members of Blue Oyster Cult:
Eric Bloom
Donald "Buck Dharma" Roeser
Richie Castellano
Jules Radino
Rudy Sarzo
and to
Sue Angle
and
Carl Bruce

Introduction: Notes Left Behind

• In August 2007, six-year-old Elena Desserich died of a rare form of brain cancer known as brainstem glioma that afflicts mostly children. Her father, Keith, said, "They told us at the very beginning that she had 135 days to live." As the brain tumor progressed, Elena lost the ability to speak, but she retained the ability to draw and to write notes to her parents and to her younger sister, Grace, to say, "I love you." Her mother, Brooke, said, "That was her way to [let] us know everything would be OK." After Elena died, her family discovered that Elena had left notes hidden in the house for them to find. Keith said that "they would be in between CDs or between books on our bookshelf. We started to collect them, and they would all say 'I love you Mom, Dad, and Grace.' We kept finding them, and still to this day, we keep finding them." Elena was clever in choosing hiding places for the notes. Keith said, "She would tuck them into bookcases, tuck them into dishes, china you don't touch every year and you'd lift it up and there'd be a note in it." Each parent has a sealed note that has never been opened. Keith explained, "We always want to know that there's one more note that we haven't read yet." Keith has written a book titled *Notes Left Behind: 135 Days with Elena* about Elena's notes. It includes the journal that he wrote during Elena's last days so that her sister Grace would have something to remember her by. Profits from the book go to the Desserichs' cancer foundation: The Cure Starts Now. Keith said, "They [readers] should take the time to listen and not get caught up in the day's rush. [...] I'll never forget that lesson. Wish I would've learned it earlier."[1]

Chapter 1: From Activism to Conductors

Activism

• In February 2011 protesters massed in Madison, Wisconsin, in response to Wisconsin's union-busting governor, Scott Walker, a Republican, who gave massive tax cuts to businesses, then declared a fiscal emergency and tried to make ordinary employees be the ones to pay for the tax cuts. His way of doing that was to remove the collective bargaining rights of many public employees. According to *New York Times* columnist Paul Krugman, some public employees — the kind who tend to be Republicans — would still retain their collective bargaining rights. Being a protester means staying on the scene for long periods of time, and of course protesters get hungry. Ian's Pizza in Madison, Wisconsin, received a request at 3:30 a.m., asking if it had any leftover pizza. It did, and so the hungry protesters got fed. Word got around that Ian's Pizza had gone above and beyond what an ordinary place of business would probably do at 3:30 a.m., and soon orders flooded in from people who wanted to order pizzas to be given to the protesters — a way of showing support for them. On Saturday, February 19, Ian's delivered more than 300 pizzas to the protesters. The calls to order pizzas for the protesters came from both near and far. The far places included Australia, Canada, China, Denmark, Egypt, Finland, Germany, Korea, the Netherlands, Turkey, and the UK. Ian's Facebook page thanked the people who wanted to feed the protesters and added, "Believe us when we say we are not really accustomed to getting pizza orders from the entire country (let alone internationally!)"[2]

• Riot Grrrl Suzy Corrigan was bullied in high school in Minneapolis, Minnesota. Fortunately, some punk girls came to her rescue by telling the bully, "If you have a problem with *her*, then we have a problem with *you*." Many of the girls in her high school were annoyed when a man started passing out anti-abortion propaganda just outside of school grounds. A few girls asked him why he was creeping around schoolgirls who were way too young for him. Many girls discovered that the propaganda could be chewed up into spitballs, which they launched at him with McDonald's straws.[3]

• When Joan Baez was 23 years old and already a successful folk singer, she publicly announced that she would no longer pay in federal income taxes the 60 percent that went to armaments. Of course, the federal government sent tax collectors to each of her concerts to get money to pay for its war machine, but at least Ms. Baez had made the government aware of her beliefs. (The government also had to spend money to collect the money — money that would otherwise have gone to armaments.)[4]

• Feminist and riot grrrl Red Chidgey performed a notable piece of activism one Valentine's Day. She set up a table as if for a dinner party complete with plates and silverware settings. On each plate she had written two things: 1) a myth of rape and 2) a reality of rape. The activism was successful: Many people worked their way around the table, reading each plate.[5]

Actors

• When Bette Davis — not widely regarded as beautiful — first arrived in Hollywood, the official greeter did not meet her. Oh, the official greeter was at the train station, but as he explained later, "No one faintly like an actress got off the train." By the way, Ms. Davis wanted to rise to the top of whatever field she was in and to be the best she could be. She once said, "If Hollywood didn't work out, I was all prepared to be the best secretary in the world."[6]

• Comedian Bert Lahr worried about other actors trying to steal a scene from him, so when he was a star other performers were under orders not to move when he was speaking. Once, he complained to a theatrical producer that a certain actor had been moving, but the producer denied that. Mr. Lahr said, "You're wrong. Tonight he was moving his facial muscles."[7]

• When Audrey Hepburn appeared as Eliza Doolittle in the movie version of *My Fair Lady*, she was made to appear dirty as the flower girl Eliza. Her costume was made to appear dirty, and it even appeared that she had dirt under her fingernails. However, Ms. Hepburn always insisted on wearing perfume although she was otherwise in character.[8]

• Sometimes Tallulah Bankhead had a weak grasp of reality, as when she said, "Cocaine isn't habit-forming. I should know — I've been using it for years." At other times, she had a firm grasp of reality; for example, in her later years, when a fan asked if she was really the "famous Tallulah," she replied, "What's left of her."[9]

• While Bob Hope was filming *The Road to Hong Kong*, he met Zsa Zsa Gabor, who told him, "Bob, darlink, I understand that there is the most vonderful part in your picture for me." Mr. Hope replied, "There sure is, honey. We'll have it written tomorrow." Then Mr. Hope told his writers to create a part for Ms. Gabor.[10]

Advertising

• The maternal grandmother of Marlo Thomas, star of TV's *That Girl*, was also the mother-in-law of Danny Thomas, star of TV's *Make Room for Daddy*. She had a beer-garden band called Marie's Merry Music Makers in which she played the drums. No fool, during the week she billed herself as "Danny Thomas's Mother-in-Law," but to get a younger crowd during the weekend she billed herself as "Marlo Thomas's Grandmother."[11]

• Adman Jerry Della Femina once wrote a best-seller titled *From Those Wonderful Folks Who Brought You Pearl Harbor*. As a young man, he had proposed that title as the slogan for a new Japanese product, but older people who were more experienced in advertising promptly shot it down. Mr. Femina also once created a controversial ad for condoms. Its slogan was this: "I enjoy sex, but I'm not willing to die for it."[12]

• Word-of-mouth advertising can work. African-American diva Ellabelle Davis (1907-1960) performed her first concert in Mexico

City in 1945. At the beginning of the concert, few people were in the audience. However, during intermission, the audience went out into the streets and told friends and neighbors that a new star had arrived. By the end of Ms. Davis' concert, the concert was standing room only.[13]

Advice

• David J. Pollay was a passenger in the back of a New York City taxicab when another car nearly caused a major collision that could have sent Mr. Pollay and the taxi driver to the hospital. The driver of the other car, who was definitely at fault, shouted obscenities at the taxi driver. However, the taxi driver simply smiled and waved at the obscenity-shouting man, and he did this without anger or sarcasm. Mr., Pollay was impressed and asked why he had done that. The taxi driver explained, "Many people are like garbage trucks. They run around full of garbage, full of frustration, full of anger, and full of disappointment. As their garbage piles up, they look for a place to dump it. And if you let them, they'll dump it on you. So when someone wants to dump on you, don't take it personally. Just smile, wave, wish them well, and move on. Believe me. You'll be happier." Mr. Pollay says, "What about you? What would happen in your life, starting today, if you let more garbage trucks pass you by? Here's my bet: You'll be happier."[14]

• An advisor to a king had to leave on an important mission. Before he left, the advisor asked the king if he would believe a man who told him that a tiger was in the street. The king replied, "No." The advisor then asked the king if he would believe two men who told him that a tiger was in the street. The king replied, "No." The advisor then asked the king if he would believe three men who told him that a tiger was in the street. This time, the king replied, "Yes." The advisor then said, "It takes the reports of only three men to convince you of something. Many more than three men are in your court. Be careful whom you believe while I am gone."[15]

• Kevin Session believes in having a good barber. According to him, "A good barber is like a good lady; once you find the right one, hold on tight." Once, his barber — a good one — changed shops. The barbers still remaining would not tell him where his barber was now working because they wanted his business. For a few weeks, he hunted for his barber, in the meantime enduring bad barbers and bad haircuts. When he finally located his barber, he told him, "Now, don't you do that again, brother. Where you go, I go."[16]

Alcohol

• The Hasidim loved Israel. Rabbi Yohanan of Rachmistrivska once owned a bottle of wine that had been bottled in Israel, but he declined to drink the wine, "I do not know whether I will like this particular bottle of wine. Since I do not want, heaven forbid, to disparage something that comes from *Eretz Israel*, I would rather not drink the bottle." Rabbi Avraham Hazan immigrated to *Eretz Israel* from Uman, and each year he would travel to Uman to celebrate Rosh Hashanah (the Jewish New Year). He always took a bottle of Israeli wine with him, and he always made sure it lasted him until he returned to Israel. Whenever he drank wine, he drank wine bottled from outside of Israel, but he put just a little of the Israeli wine in the glass so that the wine would have some of sanctity of *Eretz Israel*.[17]

• The family of William Warren Woollcott, the older brother of famous drama critic Alexander Woollcott, was at times unconventional. During the time of Prohibition, when alcoholic beverages were forbidden, Billy Woollcott made his own beer. On special occasions, he would bring up an extra bottle and let his very young daughters have a little beer along with the adults. This beer was a special treat to them. Of course, their father was a good parent. He would sometimes tell his two youngest daughters, "Drink your milk. The one who doesn't finish her milk won't get any beer tonight."[18]

• Operatic tenor Leo Slezak knew an alcoholic who called every drink an "okrepa" — that is, a strengthener — so he called the alcoholic

"Okrepa." The alcoholic spent all his money on drink, and so he never bought a railway ticket. Instead, he would arrange to be in the dining car when the ticket inspector came, and instead of purchasing a ticket, he would draw the ticket inspector into conversation and buy him drinks. Unfortunately, this always cost the alcoholic much more than simply buying the ticket would have.[19]

• Mrs. Sarah Siddons was playing Lady Macbeth on a very hot day. Being thirsty, she asked her dresser to get her a drink, so he sent a small boy to get her a glass of beer from a local pub. Returning with the beer, the boy asked where Mrs. Siddons was. Informed that she was on stage, he walked out in full view of the audience and said, "If you please, ma'am, I've brought you your beer."[20]

• Sometimes people in other countries don't quite do American things right. While in France, Peg Bracken ordered an iced tea, but after drinking half a glass, she felt like singing loudly and putting a lampshade on her head, so she asked the waiter, "Did you put gin in this?" The waiter, surprised replied, *"Mais oui, madame"* — as if to say, "Doesn't everyone?'[21]

• A dying Scotsman asked his minister if any whiskey was in Heaven. Noticing that the minister looked surprised, the dying man said, "Understand, it's not that I care for it, but it does look awfully well on the table."[22]

Animals
• In August 1996, Cerise Summers was inside her home watching a soap opera. Inside with her was Bambi, her seven-month-old pet beagle. Outside, playing in a sandbox where she could hear them, were her three-year-old son, Troy, and his playmate, Mika Paloma, who was two and a half years old. Cerise said, "At a crucial part of the program, Bambi started whining and barking to be let out. I told her to wait." Bambi would not wait. When Cerise reached out to give Bambi a swat, Bambi snapped at her — something that she had never done before. Cerise said, "I was shocked. And maybe that brainy beagle knew that

was what it would take to make me pay attention to her. Anyway, that was when I began to think seriously that something must be wrong to make her act in such a manner." Cerise let Bambi out. Cerise said, "The moment she was free of the house, she began snarling and growling like she was ready to do battle with a bear, I ran after her to see what had so upset her — and then I got the shock of my life!" The shock was a strange man who had Troy under one arm and Mika under the other. Bambi bit the man, who dropped the two children. Cerise said, "He was cursing Bambi a blue streak, but by this time I had a garden hoe in my hands and was charging toward him. He took one look at the rage in my eyes, the hoe in my hands, and the fury in Bambi's snapping teeth, and jumped over the fence. That's when I really started to scream, and several neighbors came out to see what was happening." Bambi received a very nice reward for saving the two children from the strange man: a huge serving of her favorite meal — hamburger and French fries and ketchup.[23]

• This story is from the year 2011: Regina Mayer wanted a horse, but her parents would not get her one. Therefore, the teenager, who lives on a farm in southern Germany in the hamlet of Laufen, which is very close to the Austrian border, used what was available and started riding a cow named Luna, even teaching it to jump over a hurdle. The 15-year-old Regina says about Luna, "She thinks she's a horse." Teaching Luna took many hours and many treats, but now the two take long rides together. At first, Regina simply put a halter on Luna and took her for a walk, and then gradually she got her accustomed to other riding equipment. After six months, Regina climbed up on Luna's back. Regina says, "She was really well behaved and walked normally. But after a couple of meters, she wanted me to get off! You could see that she got a bit peeved." But now Luna understands commands such as the German equivalents of "go," "stand," and "gallop." Anne Wiltafsky, a cow expert near the Swiss city of Zurich, gave Regina advice when requested. Ms. Wiltafsky says about cows, "Especially younger ones can jump really well." She also pointed out that cows can be "unbelievably devoted" to people. Martin Putzhammer, a 17-year-old neighbor of Regina, says, "At first I thought it was kind of weird — a kid on a cow? Had to get used to it, but once I did I thought it was pretty funny." Regina still hopes to get a horse one day, but she says about Luna, "She'll stay my darling."[24]

• Eric Carle, author and illustrator of the children's book *The Very Hungry Caterpillar*, loves animals. He once had a cat named Fifi, and when he was preparing string beans, he noticed that Fifi was deeply interested in the string beans. He threw a string bean down the hall, and Fifi chased it and retrieved it and begged him to throw it again. The game continued until Fifi looked tired to Mr. Carle, and then he stopped throwing the string bean. Fifi took the string bean, put it in one of Mr. Carle's shoes, and then curled around the shoe and took a nap. Each time Mr. Carle prepared string beans they played this game. And once while Mr. Carle and his wife were taking a walk to a park, they came across a turtle that was marching down a concrete sidewalk. Thinking that the sidewalk was no place for a turtle, they picked it up, carried it to the park, and released it. They then enjoyed the park. On their way back home, they came across the turtle, which was again on a sidewalk, walking toward the spot where they had first discovered it. Mr. Carle and his wife looked at each other and smiled. They picked up the turtle, carried it to the place where they had first found it, and put it down on the sidewalk. The turtle then walked to a bush and vanished.[25]

• Eric Carle, author and illustrator of many children's books, observes animals closely. At the zoo, he was watching the penguins and noticed that they were weirdly still and quiet. They were also closely observing something. Mr. Carle looked, and he saw a snake on a rock. Snakes and penguins come from different worlds, and it seemed to Mr. Carle as if the penguins were trying to figure put what a snake was and the snake was trying to figure out what penguins were. Mr. Carle told the zoo director about the snake and discovered that the snake was an escapee. The zoo director told him, "The reptile enclosure is on a different floor and quite a distance from the penguin pen. It's a mystery to me how the snake could get from one to the other." Mr. Carle went with the zoo director to the penguin pen. The zoo director saw the snake, and then he smiled and shook Mr. Carle's hand.[26]

• In Denali, Alaska, a St. Bernard named Grizzly Bear saved his owner from a real grizzly bear. Mrs. David Gratias discovered a grizzly bear cub in her backyard. Knowing that the mother grizzly bear must be near and would protect her cub, she immediately headed back to her house. Unfortunately, the mother grizzly bear was just around the corner of the house and mauled her. Fortunately, Grizzly Bear saved her life by attacking the grizzly bear, biting it and staying in between it and Mrs. Gratias, who passed out. When she awoke, Grizzly Bear was licking her face, and the grizzly bear and her cub had disappeared. Grizzly Bear was named the Ken-L Ration Dog Hero of the Year for 1970.[27]

• Syndicated columnist Connie Schultz, who lives in Ohio, remembers a group of children who attended a school near where she then lived. Each day after school they visited an orange cat named Tim-Tom. One day, Tim-Tom was not in his owners' driveway — he had died. His owners, Marianne and Paul Carey, saw the children looking for Tim-Tom, and so they posted his picture and obituary on a lamppost: "We would sadly like to let the neighborhood know that our dutiful Tim-Tom passed away on Sat. at age 18 years and 2 months. He is peacefully resting in our garden." The children wrote letters of condolence and left them under the lamppost.[28]

• P.T. Barnum once received a letter from a Vermont man offering to sell him a cherry-colored cat for $400. The letter assured him that the cat was not dyed, and that the cherry coloring was the cat's natural color. Thinking that a cherry-colored cat would be a good exhibit for his museum of curiosities, Mr. Barnum wrote out a check for $400 and mailed it. A few days later, a box arrived for Mr. Barnum. Inside the box were a black cat and a note: "In Vermont, our cherries are black."[29]

• English actress Mrs. Patrick Campbell loved Pinkie Panky Poo, her pet Pekingese, and she wanted to take him with her whenever she traveled. She once bundled him under her cloak and tried to smuggle him past customs. Later, she told her friends, "Everything was going splendidly — until my bosom barked."[30]

Birthdays

• When African-American Duke Ellington reached his 70th birthday, he celebrated it at the White House at the invitation of then-President Richard Nixon. In the receiving line, Mr. Ellington kissed each person four times — twice on each cheek. When President Nixon asked him about it, Mr. Ellington replied, "One for each cheek, Mr. President." When President Nixon gave him the Medal of Freedom at the birthday celebration, Mr. Ellington kissed him four times.[31]

• On Bernard Baruch's 95th birthday, Harry Hershfield telephoned to wish him "Happy Birthday" and to ask, "Do you think there's as much love in the world today as there was years ago?" Mr. Baruch answered, "Yes, but there's another bunch doing it."[32]

Children

• As a child, Alicia Markova saw Anna Pavlova dance — and was mesmerized. She told her father that she wanted to speak to Ms. Pavlova, so he reluctantly went backstage, where he was told to bring his daughter to her residence the next morning. Her father read the morning newspapers while Ms. Pavlova put the young Alicia through her paces. She corrected young Alicia as needed, gave her good advice — such as to take care of her teeth — and gave her a cologne rub. Finally, she warned the young Alicia that if she stayed with ballet, there was lots of hard work ahead of her. As a child, Alicia was billed as "Little Alicia, the Child Pavlova." Unfortunately, this almost kept her from being accepted as a student of the best ballet teacher in London: Serafine Astafieva. When Ms. Astafieva learned that Alicia was billed as "the Child Pavlova," she became angry because she regarded Ms. Pavlova as a supreme artist. However, young Alicia began to cry, so Ms. Astafieva allowed her to audition. Afterward, she gave Alicia a hug and told her mother, "I will accept her. Take her home. Wrap her in cotton wool — you have a racehorse."[33]

• A person who calls himself "MarkGrace" posted a funny story on the 'Kids Say the Darndest Things' thread at Cougaruteforum.com: In church some people asked little kids what they liked to do for fun. A four-year-old girl replied, "Not go to church." A man who calls himself "Clackamascoug" remembers when his little son was taking a bath and started yelling for him. He ran to the bathroom and saw his son holding a Bic razor and bleeding from a cut on his face. His son told him, "You and Mom should know better than to leave this thing where I can find it." A person by goes by the posting name "BigPiney" has a three-year-old daughter who insists that BigPiney's burps are gross but her own burps are "yummy." And "Cowboy" remembers his five-year-old praying at the dinner table: "Please bless us that we'll never, ever, ever raise our middle finger at people." By the way, Cowboy's daughter complained about her brother, "He called me fat and ugly." The brother protested: "Not fat!"[34]

• Frederick Townsend Martin was a writer and an advocate for the poor. He knew that often when rich people visited the poor they were actually slumming and snooping rather than helping. To illustrate this, he told a story about a little girl who was in a group of slum children invited to a garden party by a rich woman. The little girl asked the rich woman, "Does your husband drink?" The rich woman was shocked but replied, "Why — er — no, not to excess." The little girl then asked, "How much does he make at his job?" The rich woman explained, "He doesn't work. He's a capitalist." The little girl next asked, "You keep out of debt, I hope?" The rich woman was fed up and asked, "Look here! What do you mean by all these impudent questions?" The little girl replied, "Impudent? Why, ma'am, my mother told me to be sure and behave like a lady, and when ladies call at our rooms they always question mother like that."[35]

• Wally and his wife (who post on a "Kids Say the Darnest Things" thread) have two sons: One is three years old and the other is five years old. Being kids, and being boys, they sometimes say outrageous things. At dinner the three-year-old said, "I don't like these noodles — they taste like rotten skin." (The five-year-old, a big eater, readily ate the noodles.) The three-year-old, who is a fan of the violent comic-book character Wolverine, also said, "I am Wolverine, and I chop this bad-guy's face into a bloody stump." Wally's wife was shocked: "WHAAAAAT!" The five-year-old happily replied, "HAHAHA, BLOODY STUMP, BLOODY STUMP!" Although the kids say funny things, Wally's wife had the funniest line, which she delivered with a big sigh: "I wanted daughters *soooo* badly."[36]

• A woman who calls herself JuneBug relates that her oldest son, Erik, took his four-year-old niece downtown. JuneBug says, "Downtown is Mia's favorite place to go!" Erik and Mia did some window-shopping, and Mia picked a few flowers. Some homeless men were downtown, and Erik tried to get Mia to walk faster past the homeless men. Erik told her, "C'mon, Mia. You need to walk with me." Mia replied, "Okay, Uncle Erik, but this man needs a flower!" Mia gave the homeless man a flower, and the homeless man smiled widely. Erik says, "I'm gonna take her back downtown again soon just so she can hand out her flowers and make people smile." And JuneBug says, "Children may learn from us, but we also learn from the big hearts of our children."[37]

• According to etiquette expert Grace Fox, it is entirely appropriate for a single woman to announce the birth of her child. Ms. Fox writes in her book *Everyday Etiquette*, "The birth of a baby is always a joyous and newsworthy occasion, and I see no reason not to announce every new arrival." Women may also send separate birth announcements when separated or divorced from the father. In addition, same-sex couples who either have or adopt a child may send out announcements with the names of both partners.[38]

• Operatic tenor Leo Slezak and his wife enjoyed getting letters from their children while they were traveling on short tours. One letter from his little daughter read: "My goldfish bowl got broken when I was changing the water in the bathroom, the goldfish tumbled out and I couldn't catch him, so I filled the bathroom with water. Nanny was very cross about it, but my goldfish is all right."[39]

• As a registered nurse, Gillespie Richards has learned the correct terminology for medical conditions, and as a mother, she has learned that sometimes she ought not to use that terminology. For example, she used the correct terminology when her five-year-old son had cold sores, and he said loudly in church, "Boy, does my herpes ever hurt!"[40]

• A little girl — who said that she had experience taking ballet lessons — went to a dance class, but did nothing when the teacher ordered, "*Plié*!" Therefore, the teacher gave the English command, "Bend your knees!" To the laughter of the class, the little girl asked, "Which way?"[41]

Christmas

• In Kansas City, Missouri, a man known as Secret Santa passed out gifts of money during the Christmas season for over 25 years. That man was Larry Stewart, a millionaire (due to his cable television and long-distance telephone service) who revealed his identity after becoming seriously ill. He began giving away money in December 1979 after losing his job the week before Christmas — the second year in a row that happened to him. He was at a drive-in restaurant. He remembered, "It was cold and this car hop didn't have on a very big jacket, and I thought to myself, 'I think I got it bad. She's out there in this cold making nickels and dimes." He gave her $20 and told her to keep the change. He said, "And suddenly I saw her lips begin to tremble and tears begin to flow down her cheeks. She said, 'Sir, you have no idea what this means to me.'" Mr. Stewart went to his bank, withdrew $200, and drove around looking for people to give it to. Mr. Stewart said, "That's what we're here for — to help other people out." He died in January 2009, after reportedly giving away $1.3 million as Secret Santa. Remarkably, a new Secret Santa appeared and gave away gifts of money at Christmas, including a gift of $2,000 to retired police officer Herman Smithey III, a terminal cancer patient. Mr. Smithey said, "Around here, the word we use is 'miracle.' And that's what that was."[42]

• Following a snowfall of several inches some years ago, Eugene R. Gryniewicz asked his two sons, Joshua and Christopher, who were then in junior high school, to shovel the sidewalk, steps, and driveway, and then he would give them their allowances. After a while, he checked on them because they had not picked up their allowances, although he knew that they had planned to go to the mall with some friends who were stopping by. Investigating, he discovered that they had shoveled several sidewalks, and not just that of their own family. Indeed, some of their friends had joined them in shoveling sidewalks. However, his investigation showed that they had not approached the home dwellers to negotiate payment. One home was that of an elderly woman who took care of her bedridden nephew. Mr. Gryniewicz returned home, and soon his sons and their friends showed up. He invited everyone in for hot chocolate and cinnamon rolls, and one of his sons' friends showed him a copy of the message that they had been leaving on the doors of the houses whose sidewalks they had shoveled: "Your walk has been shoveled by the Christmas Elves. There is no need to thank us. Do something nice for someone this week. Merry Christmas. The Elves."[43]

• A person who goes by the moniker Anwahs knew a crotchety elderly man who lives near him. One winter, someone went to the elderly man's house and cleared his driveway, using the snow to make a row of smiling, waving snowmen. Because the elderly man was crotchety, he complained about the "trespasser" who had made the snowmen. Anwahs' son, however, did not know what the word "trespass" meant and thought that it must be a good thing. He was impressed by the snowmen, and exclaimed, "Wow, sir, that's the biggest, bestest present I've ever seen!" He then asked Anwahs, "Could we have someone 'trespass' on our lawn, too?" The old man smiled, and the next day he left a Christmas card outside Anwahs' front door, and he left a plush snowman as a gift for Anwahs' son. Anwahs writes that "if I ever find out who made the snowmen on [the old man's] lawn, I will be sure to send them something in return. They gave my son, myself, and our neighbor "the biggest, bestest present ever!"[44]

• Lisa Bendall has a friend named Derek who is a flight paramedic in central California. She says, "He literally saves lives in high-stress, heart-pumping emergency situations. If it sounds like a glamorous job, Derek assures me that it's both underpaid and underappreciated." He has worked in this job for 17 years and thanks are rare. However, in December 2010 Derek visited a Starbucks, and a big Texas wearing a cowboy hat was in line with him. They started talking, and when the Texan found out what Derek did for a living, he paid for Derek's coffee as well as his own. He also told Derek, sincerely, "Thank you for your public service." The Texan then wished Derek "Merry Christmas" and left. Derek says, "It's the first time anyone has ever done that kind of thing for me. I realize it wasn't about him buying me the coffee, but all about what he said." Derek also says about the good deed, "I believe I will have to pay it forward."[45]

• Duke Ellington certainly looked ahead. In early 1974 he went to the hospital because of what was his final illness. In April jazz writer and enthusiast Nat Hentoff received a Christmas card from him. Mr. Hentoff writes, "I was startled but not surprised. He always preferred to look ahead, and in case he wouldn't be around in December, he was bringing season's greetings while he could. I was depressed at what I took to be 'Goodbye.'" On May 24, Mr. Ellington died.[46]

Comedians

• Hollywood comedy writer Barney Dean was on an airplane that took him on a bouncy flight. When the plane landed and Mr. Dean was finally able to get off, he felt nauseous and asked, "You mean to tell me that Phil Harris [who had a reputation for liking alcohol] feels this way every morning?" By the way, Mr. Dean once gave a gold watch to Buddy DeSylva, head of production at Paramount. The watch was engraved: "To Buddy, this is a lot of crap, but when you don't have a lot of talent, you have to do these things, Barney."[47]

• One of Fred Allen's early ad-libs came when he was beginning a career as a juggler. His performance was very bad, and the manager of the theater came on stage and asked him, "Where did you learn to juggle?" Mr. Allen replied, "I took a correspondence course in baggage smashing."[48]

Conductors

• Sir Thomas Beecham once wanted to use a couple of French singers for a recording; however, they were not allowed to record with Sir Thomas because of the opposition of a Monsieur Hirsch, who was the Director of the Paris Opéra. This upset Sir Thomas, who was, after all, a Commandeur in the Légion d'Honneur, and thus was entitled to 12 rifle shots at his funeral. While complaining to Monsieur Varin, the Cultural Counsellor of the French Embassy, Sir Thomas requested that the 12 rifle shots at his funeral be aimed in the direction of Monsieur Hirsch.[49]

• Charles O'Connell once visited the home of Arturo Toscanini, stayed late, and then telephoned for a taxi to take him home. He told the taxi company to send a cab to the home of Mr. Toscanini, but then felt a tap on his shoulder. The great conductor reminded him, "MAESTRO, not mister."[50]

Chapter 2: From Critics to Education

Critics

• Stanley Holloway appeared as the First Gravedigger in Alec Guinness' *Hamlet*, which was not a success early in its run. Because he was not needed early in the play, he arrived late at the theater. His cabdriver once told him as he was getting out of the cab, "I wouldn't bother to go in there, if I was you. That got booed something awful on the first night." Mr. Holloway said that he had to go in the theater, as he was appearing in the play. The cabby replied, "In that case, you have my entire sympathy."[51]

• John Martin, dance critic for *The New York Times*, once wrote of Alicia Markova, "She is not only the best living ballet dancer, but probably the greatest who ever lived." Asked how she felt about such high praise, Ms. Markova replied, "It's easy to write something like that, but it's I who have to live up to it. What am I going to do the next day, I ask you? I must work all the harder. The audience is going to expect something after reading that bit. It will be hard lines if I let them down!"[52]

• Peter Wright, the director of the Sadler's Wells Royal Ballet, and ballerina Galina Samsova staged a new production of *Swan Lake* in 1981. After the work had been completed, Mr. Wright said, "The thing about the creative process is that you must hide it. You're tempting fate if you don't. You must say, 'Oh well, we'll slap a bit of paint on that,' because if you say, 'This is going to be important, great art,' God will be listening and He'll say, '*And* you'll get it wrong.'"[53]

• Olin Downes, music critic of *The New York Times*, once objected in a review to mezzo-soprano Risë Stevens' German in her appearance as Octavian in Strauss' *Der Rosenkavalier*. Finding herself seated next to Mr. Downes at a dinner party, Ms. Stevens spoke to him in German, forcing him to admit that he didn't speak German. She smiled, then said, "I do."[54]

• Egon Brecher once acted in a play in Vienna. He played a Japanese man, and in the cast were six actors who were from Japan. A critic wrote that only Mr. Brecher was convincing as a Japanese person. Mr. Brecher says, "It was true. I played the Austrian idea of a Japanese."[55]

Dance

• Rudolf Nureyev valued his freedom. In 1961, he was on tour with the Kirov Ballet in France, when he was suddenly told at the airport that although the rest of the Kirov Ballet would fly to London, he was to fly to Russia. Sensing that if he returned to Russia, he would never again be allowed to dance in the West, Mr. Nureyev immediately approached two French policemen in the airport and demanded their protection. After Rudolf Nureyev defected to the West from the Soviet Union, he began to dance with Margot Fonteyn. At first, Ms. Fonteyn resisted the idea. She was much older than Mr. Nureyev and felt, "It would be like mutton dancing with lamb." However, she and her husband discussed the idea of the dance partnership. They decided that Mr. Nureyev would be the next great sensation in ballet and for the benefit of her career, Ms. Fonteyn decided to dance with him. Despite (or because of) the practical nature of her decision, it was a wise one, and the two dancers blossomed artistically together.[56]

• When Shirley Temple first met Bill "Bojangles" Robinson, she asked if she could call him "Uncle Billy." Mr. Robinson replied, "Why, sure you can. But then I get to call you 'darlin.'" They made the deal, and they starred together in four movies. When they danced in their four movies together, they used a hand squeeze system. Three squeezes meant that a hard part was coming up. One long squeeze meant, "Really good, darlin.'" No squeeze meant, "Well, let's do it again." Of course, Shirley Temple did a lot of tap dancing in her movies. Whenever one of her movies came out, parents would see it, then enroll their children in classes to learn tap dancing. Gene Kelly used to say that enrollment at his dance schools would nearly quadruple whenever a new Shirley Temple movie came out.[57]

• As a young dancer, Alicia Marks, who later danced under the name of Alicia Markova, was taken to audition for Princess Seraphine Astafieva. Alicia's mother stopped by Ms. Astafieva's dance studio one day and sent in a card announcing "Little Alicia — The Child Pavlova." Big mistake. Ms. Astafieva believed that Pavlova was a great artist, and she was very angry that anyone would dare to bill a small child as "The Child Pavlova." Nevertheless, Ms. Astafieva watched little Alicia audition, then took her on as a student. Alicia's mother immediately burned the offending cards in the fireplace. However, a short time later Ms. Astafieva presented the small dance student at a concert as "Little Alicia — The Miniature Pavlova."[58]

• Anna Pavlova and her dance company performed all over the world. In Mexico City, they danced on a stage in the bullring. This created a problem because it often rained in the afternoons when they danced. Ms. Pavlova was once amused to see her music director, Theodore Stier, conduct while a large umbrella was held over him. She knew the laws of the many countries she danced in. In Mexico, there was a law saying that if an open-air performance stopped within a certain length of time, the admission price would have to be refunded to the audience. As Ms. Pavlova danced, a heavy downpour began and her company rushed to get under shelter, but mindful of the law, she continued dancing and finished the performance.[59]

• In George Balanchine's "Apollo," the great choreographer has Apollo appear to walk on his knees. When a reporter questioned Mr. Balanchine's choreography, asking when he had seen Apollo walk on his knees, Mr. Balanchine replied by asking when the reporter had seen Apollo. The great choreographer also has Apollo alternatively open and close his hands a number of times. Mr. Balanchine claimed that the movement originated from the blinking advertising signs he had seen in London's Piccadilly Circus. (One Apollo he had personally coached claimed that Mr. Balanchine had told him that the opening and closing of the hands meant "Bar and grill! Bar and grill!")[60]

• Ballet student Alice Patelson was taking a class with Pierre Vladimiroff, who ended his lessons by ordering his class to perform 32 *fouettés* in a row — a difficult maneuver in which the ballerina turns around on one foot while whipping the other leg. After expertly completing the maneuver, Ms. Patelson rested at the barre while the rest of the class worked on perfecting their *fouettés*. Mr. Vladimiroff came over to the barre and complimented her *fouettés*: "You are not working; you are dancing."[61]

• Early in her career, New York City Ballet ballerina Suzanne Farrell rehearsed *Movements* with music by Igor Stravinsky. Afterward, she went up to choreographer George Balanchine and said, "I don't think you should let me do this ballet. I'm just not ready for it." Mr. Balanchine simply told her, "You let me be the judge." Later, she learned that during the rehearsal, Mr. Stravinsky had asked who she was. Mr. Balanchine had replied, "Igor Fyodorovich, this is Suzanne Farrell. Just been born."[62]

• In dance class, Daniel Nagrin was suddenly asked by another dancer, "What are you *really* going to do?" Mr. Nagrin answered, "I'm going to dance!" The woman asked, "Why?" This caused Mr. Nagrin to think about what other choreographers were doing, and then he said, "Because I'm going to be dealing with things that the others aren't going to touch!" His career proved this true. Mr. Nagrin became a loner of dance, who has performed solo dance concerts everywhere.[63]

• While taking dance classes, Alice Patelson studied both ballet and modern dance. No matter who taught the ballet classes, at the end of the lesson she ended up with sore feet. The modern dance class was different. Her teacher, Janet Collins, had the class sit on the floor, then perform various exercises and movements — so at the end of the modern dance class Ms. Patelson ended up with a sore bottom.[64]

• Ballerina Alicia Markova was known for her arabesque — a position in which the ballerina arches her spine and raises one leg, all while balancing on pointe on a straight leg. When Agnes de Mille was watching a performance by Ms. Markova, she overheard an elderly gentleman exclaim on seeing Ms. Markova's arabesque, "It is not possible, but I see it with my eyes, so she must be doing it!"[65]

• While dancing in the Philippines, Alicia Markova and Anton Dolin rigged up a stage and taught a couple of Filipino men to work the lights, changing the color as needed. However, the lights remained blue throughout the entire performance — the Filipino men were so entranced by the dancing on stage that they completely forgot about the lights.[66]

• In *Blackbirds of 1928*, the great dancer Bill Robinson, aka Mr. Bojangles, performed his famous stair dance on Broadway. After the Broadway run, he declined to go on the road with the show and was replaced by Eddie Rector. One day, Mr. Rector received a telegram from Mr. Bojangles: "DO MY STAIR DANCE AND YOU DIE."[67]

• Choreographer George Balanchine was criticized because he hired black dancer Arthur Mitchell. In reply, Mr. Balanchine said, "You must understand that Negro blood or Japanese blood or Russian blood doesn't mean a thing to me. I don't take people because they are black or white. I take *exquisite* people — people who are made to dance."[68]

• At the housewarming party for her home at Hampstead, Anna Pavlova hired dancers to represent gnomes and nymphs. They danced for a while, then they circled a tree and danced around it. Ms. Pavlova dropped out of the tree, and in a magical moment, she danced "The Sylph."[69]

• As a very young dance pupil — 14 years old — Margot Fonteyn (then known as Margaret Hookham) showed much ambition. When she was told that Ms. Pavlova was the "greatest dancer in the world," she replied, "Then I will be the second greatest."[70]

Death

• Nicholas Green, a seven-year-old boy from Bodega Bay, California, was shot in the head by highway robbers in Italy; two days later, he died. His parents, Reg and Maggie, donated his organs to seven Italians and saved or vastly improved their lives. This led to an awareness of the importance of organ donation, and many, many people are alive or are living better lives because so many people heard of Nicholas Green and decided to donate their organs. His parents call this the "Nicholas Effect." His father even wrote a book titled *The Nicholas Effect: A Young Boy's Gift to the World*. In a 1999 online chat, Reg explained why he and his wife made the decision to donate Nicholas's organs: "When we looked at Nicholas, he didn't look like a sleeping child. We knew he was dead and therefore didn't need that body anymore. But he'd been in perfect health, so that body can help other people, and as it turned out it was seven very sick people." He added, "We can't remember ever having heard a conversation about organ donation, but when we saw Nicholas that day, it seemed perfectly obvious to us that this was the right thing to do. His future had been taken away from him. It seemed even more important than ever that that future should be given to someone else. In fact, all seven of those Italian recipients are now back in the mainstream of life." Reg and Meg have met all of the people to whom their son's organs were donated. Reg said, "All of them are living normal lives. One woman had never seen her baby's face clearly but now has regained her sight. The two children who had spent hours a day, three days a week, hooked up to dialysis machines are now perfectly normal youngsters. The boy who got Nicholas's heart had previously had six operations on his own heart and all had failed. Now he's like any normal boy. The woman who got Nicholas's pancreas cells was a diabetic and had been repeatedly in comas. She was completely dependent on others. The last time I saw her, she was living alone for the first time. And then there was the 19-year-old girl who received Nicholas's liver, and she [had been] going to die, and the family had gathered to say goodbye. But with the new liver, she came back to good health, was married, and last year had a baby. It was a boy, and they have called him Nicholas." Organ donation helps to reveal the "unity of mankind," Reg said, pointing out, "When organs are donated, you do not know who will receive them. White men are walking around with black women's hearts in them. Anglos are breathing with Mexican lungs. American children are being saved by the organs of Italians and vice versa in all of those cases. The differences between us as human beings are trifling compared to what we have in common."[71]

• Harry Cohn, the head of Columbia Pictures, was Jewish, but his wife says that he converted to Christianity on his deathbed. His friend the comedian Danny Thomas was known for being religious, so Mrs. Cohn telephoned him to see if he was willing to read the prayers at her husband's funeral. She explained, "I don't want to have a rabbi, and I don't want to insult his family by having a priest." Mr. Thomas is a nice guy, but he knew that Mr. Cohn was Jewish, and he wondered whether a Christian like himself should read the prayers. Mrs. Cohn said, "Let me tell you something, When Harry was dying, he said, 'Jesus, help me!' I'm a Christian, as you know, and I'm sure he was turning to Jesus in his final moments." Mr. Thomas was still skeptical, and he asked, "Are you sure he wasn't just exclaiming, 'Jesus Christ,' like we all do in tense moments?" Mrs. Cohn replied, "I knew him a little better than you. I shared his bed, and I'm telling you he said, 'Jesus, help me.' So I went and got a glass of water, sprinkled it on him, and I said, 'I baptize you in the name of the Father, the Son, and the Holy Ghost.' Now, will you please say the prayers over him at the grave site?" Mr. Thomas agreed, but he consulted a wise man, Monsignor Concannon, the pastor of the Church of the Good Shepherd in Beverly Hills. The good Monsignor gave him the funeral book, and told him, "Wherever it says 'Jesus Christ,' you substitute the word 'Lord' — meaning the Lord God of us all. That way, you will not offend anyone." Mr. Thomas did exactly that, and he recited the Twenty-third Psalm, and no one was offended. Yes, Monsignor Concannon is a wise man.[72]

• *Shoah*, a 1985 movie, is an over-nine-hour-long witness to the Holocaust. Among the people appearing in the movie are Nazis, survivors, and bystanders. One person interviewed is the survivor Filip Muller, a Jew who watched other Jews walk into a gas chamber to die. He watched and listened as a group of Czech Jews sang two songs as they walked into the gas chamber. One song — "The Hatikvah" — affirmed that they were Jewish. The other song — the Czech national anthem — affirmed that they were Czech. Mr. Muller says, "They denied Hitler, who would have them be one but not the other." Mr. Muller felt that he had no reason to go on living, so he went inside the gas chamber with them. However, a small group of women came over to him, and one woman said, "So you want to die. But that's senseless. Your death won't give us back our lives. That's no way. You must get out of here alive, you must bear witness to our suffering and to the injustice done to us." In his review of this movie — a Great Movie — Roger Ebert writes, "And that is the final message of this extraordinary film. It is not a documentary, not journalism, not propaganda, not political. It is an act of witness. In it, [filmmaker] Claude Lanzmann celebrates the priceless gift that sets man apart from animals and makes us human, and gives us hope: the ability for one generation to tell the next what it has learned."[73]

• On Groucho Marx' *You Bet Your Life* TV quiz show, some of the guests were as entertaining as Groucho. For example, the Reverend James Whitcomb Broughter, a Baptist minister, told about getting dressed for a benefit. He had trouble tying his bowtie, so when the man who was going to take him to the banquet room showed up, he asked him if he knew how to tie it. The man did know, and he asked Reverend Broughter to lie down on the bed and then he tied the bowtie. Reverend Broughter asked, "Why did you make me lie down on the bed?" The man replied, "That's the only way I can do it. I'm an undertaker." By the way, when Groucho had just agreed to be the host of the *You Bet Your Life* quiz show, which started on radio, and then later moved to TV, he objected when he heard that one of the writers, Bernie Smith, was being paid $300 a week: "He can't be any good. You can't get a good writer for less than $900 a week." John Guedel, the executive producer of *You Bet Your Life*, took the criticism seriously. He called Mr. Smith into his office, fired him, and then rehired him at $900 a week.[74]

• In early 2011, Charles Nolan, a fashion designer and the significant other of finance writer Andrew Tobias, died. Before he died, he had a goal that he wished to achieve. The hallway that he shared with two neighbors was ugly, and Mr. Nolan hated ugly. Mr. Tobias writes that "a few weeks ago, Charles took charge. Designs were designed, frames framed, contractors contracted with, carpet squares ordered. Two weeks ago today, he said, 'I know this is going to sound ridiculous, but I don't want to die until they finish the hallway.'" After briefly considering asking the contractors to slow down, but realizing that both he and Mr. Nolan knew that it was the right time for Mr. Nolan to die (except for the hallway), Mr. Tobias spoke to the contractors, who had seemed to him to be working slowly, and remarkably the entire job was finished in the next two days. Mr. Tobias says that the hallway went from being "the ugliest hallway in the building, possibly in the entire neighborhood" to being "the sharpest hallway in the building, possibly the entire neighborhood."[75]

• George Jessel was known as the Toastmaster of the United States because he spoke at so many dinners and gave so many elegies at funerals. He once observed a number of veterans at a dining room in a hotel. They had fought together, and some had been injured in battle, including a man who could no longer speak. At the table was an empty chair for one of their fellows who had been killed in battle. One by one they made a toast to their fallen comrade and drank. When it was his turn to make a toast, the veteran who could not speak stood up, raised a glass to the empty chair, then sat down, and all drank. Mr. Jessel says, "It was the most eloquent toast I've ever witnessed."[76]

• A gunfight was once averted because of money. During the Alaskan gold rush, a man named Jack McCloud lost all his money in a poker game at Tex Rickard's Great Northern, a bar and gambling place. Feeling cheated, he challenged Mr. Rickard to a gunfight. Mr. Rickard checked the condition of his gun, then thought about his net worth. If he lost the gunfight, he would lose his life and $300,000. If he won the gunfight, Mr. McCloud would lose only his life. After thinking it over, Mr. Rickard ordered a friend, "Tell Jack I can't afford it. Here I am, worth three hundred thousand, and he's broke. I won't stack that up against nothing. It ain't business."[77]

• When Sam Kinison died, lots of comedians showed up at his funeral and talked about him. Richard Belzer emceed, and Pauly Shore talked about how Sam used to be his babysitter. Comedian (and Sam's best friend) Carl Labove had been with Sam when he died, and he spoke — but briefly, as he started to cry. Mr. Belzer helped him from the podium and led him to a chair, but suddenly Mr. Labove broke away from Mr. Belzer, ran back to the podium, and announced, "By the way, I'll be at Iggy's all week! Two shows Friday, three Saturday!" I'm sure that Sam would have loved it.[78]

• As a young ballet dancer in the Soviet Union, Natalia Makarova had an especially difficult time dancing the Czar-maiden in Cesar Pugni's *Humpbacked Horse*. Once, just before the last variation, she became hysterical off-stage because of the difficulty of the role, and started shouting, "I won't go back onstage for anything! You want me dead!" She then grabbed a handrail and held on. Natalia Dudinskaya and Seva Ukhov somehow pulled her off the handrail and pushed her onto the stage, where she finished the dance. Later, Ms. Makarova became a world-class ballerina.[79]

• Country music singer Willie Nelson has a lot of respect for Dr. Red Duke, but since mortals are in fact mortal, even the best doctors will have some patients — especially old patients — die. Dr. Duke took care of Willie's mother before she died, and he took care of Willie's father-in-law before he died, so Mr. Nelson joked, "If you don't quit losing them, I'm going to quit sending them to you." Dr. Duke smiled and said, "Willie, you're just going to have to get them to me earlier."[80]

• King Louis XI condemned to death the champion archer of France, John de Roche, but he gave him a chance to win his freedom by making a difficult shot. Mr. de Roche thought about the offer for a moment, then said, "Sire, under these conditions I am liable to miss and ruin my reputation." He preferred definitely losing his head to the guillotine to possibly losing his reputation.[81]

• Jan Murray was a funny comedian, but he was a klutz around the house. Whenever anything went wrong with the electrical wiring or plumbing, Mrs. Murray fixed it. When his friend the comedian Buddy Hackett's father died, Jan telephoned Buddy to give his condolences and to find out about the funeral. Ever the comedian, Buddy joked, "Don't come. You'll fall in the hole."[82]

• After Oscar Wilde was released from prison after serving two years, he went to Paris, where he saw a palm reader. She looked at his palm, inspected the line that indicated how long he would live, and then said, "By your line of life you died two years ago. I cannot explain the fact except by supposing that since then you have been living on the line of your imagination."[83]

• While fashion designer Pauline Trigère was dining in a restaurant, a man approached her to tell her that his mother, one of her longtime customers, had been buried in one of her creations. Ms. Trigère told her dining companions, "You see! With a Trigère you can go anywhere!"[84]

• Donald Ogden Stewart once told a harrowing story to a society lady about how his sloop had been capsized and he had to struggle for his life and was in danger of drowning near the Clews' house — at this point the society lady interrupted by asking, "How *are* the Clews?"[85]

• According to etiquette expert Grace Fox, if you are choking, you should not leave the table. You may need someone to perform the Heimlich maneuver on you and save your life. (It's impolite to choke to death at a dinner party or a restaurant.)[86]

• While traveling abroad, Mark Twain read newspapers reports that he had died, so he sent this telegram to the Associated Press: "The reports of my death are greatly exaggerated."[87]

Education

• On 26 February 1993, a terrorist bomb exploded in the underground parking garage beneath the World Trade Center in New York. Among the people on the 107th floor of the South Tower were nearly 100 children from the five kindergarten classes at Brooklyn's Public School 95. Three classes of children made it down the elevator safely before the bomb exploded. Anna Marie Tesoriero and her class of children, as well as other passengers and a few parents, were in the elevator when the bomb exploded. The elevator stopped, and four hours later they were rescued. Still on the 107th floor was Rosemarie Russo with her class of kindergartners. Smoke began to fill the air, and Ms. Russo and her class and the other people on the 107th floor went to the roof, five floors higher, for fresh air. The children interlocked their arms and climbed the escalators, which of course were no longer running. A light snow was falling, and Ms. Russo kept the children close to a wall for shelter from the wind. Some people around them gave Ms. Russo some clothing — a coat, some gloves, and scarves — to help keep the children warm. Ms. Russo said, "One of my little girls was wearing patent leather shoes and anklets, and a man who worked in the building picked her up and put her on his shoulders so her feet wouldn't get cold from the snow." Ms. Russo was an experienced teacher, and she had brought a shopping bag filled with supplies, including lollipops, popcorn, pretzels, and raisins, because, she said,

"You never know with kids." She passed out the treats. She also had the children sing songs as they waited. Ms. Russo says about her students, "They were fine. They forgot about the emergency; they forgot about the cold." Hours later, the smoke had cleared, and everyone on the roof was able to begin walking down the stairs to street level — over 100 stories. Two firefighters used their axes to break the glass door of a gift shop and take out boxes of small souvenir penlights. Each kindergartner got a penlight to help light the way down the dark stairs. Ms. Russo said that while the penlights were being passed out, "They [the kindergartners] played all kinds of games with them. They used them to play dentist and look in one another's mouths. They looked in one another's ears." Then they started walking down the stairs. Once they reached the 95th floor, they stopped to eat a snack of cookies, milk, and juice at tables that emergency workers had set up. Then they started walking down the stairs again. Usually, the children counted each step on a flight of stairs — 20 stairs to each flight. Ms. Russo says about her students, "It was an adventure for them." At the bottom of each flight, Ms. Russo, who led the way down, called to her educational assistant, Dorothy Byrd, who brought up the rear, "Everything OK, Dorothy?" She also checked with the parents who were present. In addition, firefighters and other emergency personnel often checked in with the group to see if everything was OK. The floors were numbered, and so Ms. Russo always knew how many floors were left to go down. She would tell the children things such as, "Just 67 more. Not far. Not far." Finally, they reached the street level. The children shouted, "We made it! We made it!" Climbing down the stairs from the roof had taken two and one-half hours. Ms. Tesoriero and Ms. Russo and their classes took the same bus back to Public School 95, where the children were reunited with happy parents. One mother said, "My son can go to the Bronx Zoo or the Botanical Gardens, to concerts or shows, but nothing with an elevator."[88]

• Sister Helen P. Mrosla, a Franciscan nun, taught Mark Eklund in the third grade at Saint Mary's School in Morris, MN, and she taught him again in a math course in the ninth grade. One day, the students were struggling in class, and she decided to do something different to stop their bad spirits and crankiness. She asked each student to take out some paper and list each classmate's name on it, leaving some room in between each name. She then asked students "to think of the nicest thing they could say about each of their classmates and write it down." At the end of the class, she collected the papers. Over the weekend, she wrote down the name of each student on a separate sheet and then she wrote down on each sheet of paper the nice comments that the other students had written about that student. On Monday, she gave each student his or her list of nice comments. She remembers, "Before long, the entire class was smiling. 'Really?' I heard whispered. 'I never knew that meant anything to anyone!' 'I didn't know others liked me so much!" No one ever mentioned those papers in class again. I never knew if they discussed them after class or with their parents, but it didn't matter. The exercise had accomplished its purpose. The students were happy with themselves and one another again." A few years later, in 1971, a grown-up Mark Eklund died in Vietnam — not in combat, but from a pulmonary and cerebral edema while sleeping. Sister Helen attended his funeral, and a soldier who was a pallbearer asked her, "Were you Mark's math teacher?" He then said, "Mark talked about you a lot." And Mark's father said to her, "We want to show you something. They found this on Mark [...]. We thought you might recognize it." The something was the piece of paper on which Sister Helen had written a list of students' nice comments about Mark. The well-worn paper had obviously been read often. Mark's mother said, "Thank you so much for doing that. As you can see, Mark treasured it." Several other students who had been in the class, including Mark's wife, kept their own lists of nice comments. One former student showed

Sister Helen her list and said, "I carry this with me at all times. I think we all saved our lists."[89]

• Don't fear the reaper, but try not to throw away your life needlessly. The ancient people of Japan passed on what they had learned from their experiences of tsunamis. Those who heeded the wisdom of the ancient people fared better in the great tsunami of 2011 than those who did not. For example, in the village of Aneyoshi, a stone slab that is hundreds of years old stated, "High dwellings are the peace and harmony of our descendants. Remember the calamity of the great tsunamis. Do not build any homes below this point." The people of Aneyoshi had not built any homes below that point, and they fared well in the earthquake. On the coastline of Japan, hundreds of stone slabs bear good advice. For example, a stone slab states, "If an earthquake comes, beware of tsunamis." Another stone slab states, "Always be prepared for unexpected tsunamis. Choose life over your possessions and valuables." Such advice is needed. Large tsunamis occur rarely, and without such reminders, people can forget the danger and do such things as build homes on the coastline — as many people in other areas of Japan had done. Tetsuko Takahashi, 70, who lived in a hillside house in Kesennuma, saw from her window a ship swept inland a half-mile — it crushed buildings as it was swept inland. She said, "After the earthquake, people went back to their homes to get their valuables [...]. They all got caught." The names of towns also provide warnings. For example, one town is named "Octopus Grounds" because a tsunami once washed onto it lots of sea life. Fumihiko Imamura, a professor in disaster planning at Tohoku University, said, "It takes about three generations for people to forget. Those that experience the disaster themselves pass it to their children and their grandchildren, but then the memory fades." In Aneyoshi, people remembered. Yuto Kimura, who was 12 years old, said, "Everybody here knows about the markers. We studied them in school. When the tsunami came, my mom got me from school and then the whole village climbed to higher ground."[90]

• Tilly Smith, a 10-year-old English schoolgirl, saved approximately 100 people at a resort on the Thai island of Phuket from a tsunami on 26 December 2004. The tsunami killed at least 178,000 people. Fortunately for the people at the resort, Tilly had studied tsunamis in her geography class in Oxshott, a small town south of London, just two weeks earlier. Tilly said, "I saw this bubbling on the water, right on the edge, and foam sizzling just like in a frying pan. The water was coming in, but it wasn't going out again. It was coming in, and then in, and then in, towards the hotel." Tilly told her mother, Penny, "Mum, I know there's something wrong. I know it's going to happen — the tsunami." Her mother did not believe her at first. However, her father, Colin, said, "Tilly went hysterical." Colin and Tilly's eight-year-old sister, Holly, went to the hotel and spread news of the approaching tsunami, and Tilly told a Japanese-born hotel chef who recognized the word "tsunami." The chef and a hotel security agent helped spread the news of the approaching tsunami at the beach, and people left the beach. Minutes later, the tsunami hit the beach. According to media reports, "The beach near the Marriott Hotel was one of the few in Phuket where no one was killed or seriously hurt." Former United States President Bill Clinton met with Tilly the following year. He said, "Tilly's story is a simple reminder that education can make a difference between life and death. All children should be taught disaster reduction so they know what to do when natural hazards strike." Because of Tilly, many people lived through the tsunami who otherwise would have died. Fortunately for them, Tilly likes studying geography.[91]

• After Joe Hyams tried tricky moves against a more skillful sparring partner — and got beat — kenpo-karate master Ed Parker spoke to him. Mr. Parker drew a line on the floor with chalk and asked, "How can you shorten the line?" Mr. Hyams gave several answers, all of which Mr. Parker rejected. Mr. Parker then drew a second, longer line and asked, "How does the first line look?" Of course, in comparison with the long, second line, the first line looked shorter. Mr. Parker then said, "It is always better to improve and strengthen your own line or knowledge than to try and cut your opponent's line." After that, Mr. Hyams tried to improve his own knowledge and skills instead of trying to trick his opponent.[92]

• On a cold winter Sunday several people went to church. Outside the front door of the church was a man who appeared to be homeless and sleeping. A hat was pulled over his eyes, so no one was able to see his face. His overcoat was very old and very worn, and his shoes had holes. No one invited the man into the church, and no one offered to help him. Instead, worshippers walked by him and went into the church. When services were scheduled to start, the "homeless" man walked into the church, went to the altar, and took off his hat. The "homeless" man was the church's preacher, who told the congregation, "Folks, I don't think I have to tell you what I am preaching about today."[93]

• Anne Fine, author of *Alias Madame Doubtfire*, had a good teacher at age nine. Each Monday, Mr. Simpson would write five titles on the chalkboard and tell his students to write a story. He criticized each story with comments such as, "Well, what happened to that spaceship?" and "I think that you forgot that you had a princess on page two." Ms. Fine says that "it was amazing practice to be left alone to do this every week, learning how many characters you can take on board and still sort out tidily by the end."[94]

• Ruth Bader Ginsburg was very busy as a law professor and as an ACLU lawyer, but whenever James, her young son, got into trouble at school, the school principal always called her and not her husband. Finally, she informed the principal that James had two parents — not one — and she requested that the principal call her husband half of the time when James got into trouble at school. In 1993, Ms. Ginsburg became a Justice of the United States Supreme Court.[95]

• An engineering professor gave his class this question on a final exam: Using a barometer and any other tools you wish, how would you measure the height of a building? Note: You must use the barometer." Only one student gave the correct answer: "I would climb to the top of the building, tie the barometer to a piece of string, lower the barometer to the ground, then I would measure the length of the string. This would tell me the height of the building."[96]

• The first dance choreographed by George Balanchine that ballerina Illaria Obidenna Ladré ever saw was performed by Mr. Balanchine and Olga Mungalova to Arthur Rubenstein's "Night." Because she was a young dancer studying with other young dancers, and because the choreography was very daring, Illaria and her classmates were forbidden to watch the rehearsals — so of course they all did.[97]

• In the 5th grade, his teacher asked Jon Scieszka, "What's so funny?" Jon replied with a story about a man who had no arms but made his living as a bell-ringer by hitting the bell with his head. Someone asked, "What's that guy's name?" Someone else answered, "I don't know, but his face sure rings a bell." The students laughed; the teacher didn't.[98]

• Influential dance teacher Nicolas Legat knew and studied under Marius Petipa, the choreographer of *Swan Lake*. Mr. Legat described Mr. Petipa's "system" in this way: "To look for beauty, grace, and simplicity, and obey no other rules."[99]

Chapter 3: From Fans to Media

Fans

• Dolly Parton respects her fans, and she wears full makeup even when she is traveling to a photo shoot at which she knows that her makeup will be immediately removed and reapplied. Makeup artist extraordinaire Kevyn Aucoin once asked her why she did that, and she replied, "I have to look my best at all times for my fans — what if I'm in a car accident?"[100]

• In the days of American slavery, General George Washington was walking down the street when an aged African-American saw him and took off his hat and bowed out of respect. General Washington promptly took off his hat and returned the bow. Later, he explained to a shocked white politician: "I cannot be less civil than a poor Negro."[101]

• Bob Denver played Gilligan on *Gilligan's Island*, a role that has followed him ever since. While he was vacationing on Hawaii, a Hawaiian family found out where he was staying and sang the *Gilligan's Island* theme song outside his window at 6 a.m. until he woke up and said hi.[102]

Fathers

• Roger Ebert's father, whom Roger called "Daddy," used to tell a story that he had learned from his own father. The story was about an immigrant from Germany to this country. In the old country, he had learned the English words "coffee" and "apple pie." At a restaurant, he ordered apple pie, and when the server asked if he wanted anything on top of it, he said, "Coffee." Roger started writing early for a newspaper. Before he was in his junior year of high school, he got a job covering the Urbana Tigers for *The News-Gazette* even though this meant that he had to work until 1 or 2 a.m. a couple of nights a week, and he had to drive home by himself. Roger was good at the job, and he won the Illinois Associated Press sportswriting contest for an article that he wrote during his senior year of high school. When Roger's father lay dying of cancer in a hospital bed, Roger took him the framed certificate that he had received for winning the contest. Although Roger later won a Pulitzer Prize for his movie criticism, he says about the award that he took to his dying father, "It was the most important prize I ever won." During one visit to the hospital, following his father's surgery, Roger saw his father and mother do and say something that he is grateful to have seen and heard. Roger writes, "He sat up on the edge of his bed. 'Hold me, Bub,' he said. 'It hurts so much.' She took him in her arms. 'Oh, Wally,' she said, 'I love you so much.'"[103]

• On Father's Day, Danny Thomas' young children gave him cards. Daughter Marlo gave him a funny card, which he read out loud and enjoyed. Daughter Terre then gave him a sentimental card that described him as "the best father in the world" and as "caring and loving." Danny liked the card and read it out loud, but he asked Terre, "Do you believe all of this?" Terre answered, "Yes, Daddy." Danny then said, "Because if you really believed what's written in this card, you'd do the things Daddy wants you to do, wouldn't you?" Again, Terre said, "Yes, Daddy." Danny continued, "Like right now. Where's your retainer?" Terre answered, "It's upstairs, Daddy." Danny said, "Upstairs! I didn't spend my hard-earned money for you to put your retainer in a drawer upstairs! It belongs in your mouth! I bought it for you so you would grow up to have beautiful straight teeth, with a smile to be proud of!" Terre looked at Marlo and said, "You couldn't have given me the other card?" Sometimes, the children of professional comedians as just as funny as the professional comedians.[104]

Food

• Ann Cooper gave up her 30-plus-year career as a chef to start cooking healthy meals for schoolchildren in Berkeley, California. She prepares roast chicken, not chicken nuggets, and she prepares roast potatoes, not Tater Tots. In addition to this work, she wrote a book titled *Lunch Lessons: Changing the Way We Feed Our Children*. All of this is an effort to reform school lunches to make them healthy. The lunches she prepares are seasonal, fresh, and mostly organic, as opposed to frozen, fried, and sugary. She says, "I want to change children's relationship to food." As director of nutrition services for the Berkeley Unified School District, she ensures that 95 percent of the cafeteria food is made from scratch. Previously, 95 percent of the cafeteria food was processed. Some students were resistant to eating the healthy food at first. She says, "I have received hate mail. Kids speak up if they don't like something." Some fifth-graders even told her, "Ms. Cooper, we hate your food. We're going on a hunger strike." They told her that they especially disliked her grilled-cheese sandwiches, which were made from whole-wheat bread and cheddar cheese. She invited them into the kitchen and taught them how to make bread and gave them various kinds of cheeses to taste. Eventually, their taste buds developed, and they told the next group of fifth-graders, "You are so lucky. We fixed all the food here for you."[105]

• When Trisha Yearwood married Garth Brooks, she began living in Oklahoma instead of Georgia — thus the title of her cookbook *Georgia Cooking in an Oklahoma Kitchen* — and only once did she feel really, really homesick. That was when she had the flu and her mother was not there to take care of her. Her mother made chicken noodle soup, froze it, and mailed it to her in a Styrofoam container packed with dry ice. Trisha says, "When I got it the next morning, I cried, ate some soup, cried, ate some more soup, and thanked God for the most awesome mom on the planet!" (Now, Oklahoma as well as Georgia feels like home to her.) By the way, Trisha's first home-cooked meal for Garth was Fettuccine Alfredo, and it did not turn out the way it was supposed to — the sauce was way, way too thick. Trisha says that she is surprised that Garth ever allowed her to cook another meal, although being a gentleman he took a huge serving. (The meal was so rich that he almost fell asleep at the dinner table, and he says he does not remember anything from being halfway through the meal to waking up a few hours later on the couch.)[106]

• The Methodist circuit riders worked hard, and they developed hardy appetites — especially for chicken, as everyone knew. Every time a circuit rider stayed for supper, the farmwife would kill one or two fat chickens. This joke illustrates the reputation and appetite that Methodist circuit riders had for eating chicken: One day a circuit rider was on a bridge when he dropped his false teeth, which fell into the water. A young boy who was fishing asked the circuit rider where he had eaten that day. The place was close, so the boy told the circuit rider to wait a while and then he would get his teeth for him. The boy left, then returned quickly, carrying a chicken bone with him. He tied the chicken bone to his fishing line, then he cast it into the water. A few seconds later, he drew the fishing line out of the water. At the end of the fishing line was the circuit rider's false teeth — clamped tight on the chicken bone.[107]

• In Trinidad, ballet dancer Alexandra Danilova decided to try passion fruit, something she had never eaten before, and so she asked her friend and fellow ballet dancer Alicia Markova to buy her some in the marketplace. Unfortunately, once she had the passion fruit, she didn't know how to eat it. Ms. Markova passed on the advice she had received from the vendor: "You know what the man told me? He said to take off all your clothes, get into a nice warm bath, and eat the fruit." Ms. Danilova followed the advice, which was good because she got the juice all over herself. However, she had been expecting it to be good advice for a different reason.[108]

• World-famous choreographer Leonide Massine was also famous for his appetite. Once, he stayed at a hotel where the meals were included with the price of the rooms. Unfortunately, once the proprietors discovered how much Mr. Massine ate, they were not happy. One of the proprietors even said to ballerina Alexandra Danilova about Mr. Massine, *"Mademoiselle, ce n'est pas possible — il mange tout — il gorge tout le menu.*" ("Mademoiselle, it is not possible. He eats everything; he stuffs himself on the whole menu.") Eventually, the proprietors made Mr. Massine pay extra.[109]

• When Molly Ringwald's oldest daughter entered kindergarten, all of the children were asked on their first day of school what was their favorite food. Half of the children answered "sushi" and one child answered "seaweed," and Molly was afraid that she and her husband would be branded "the world's worst parents" because their daughter, a picky eater, loved to eat something that Molly describes as "cheese-dusted packaged air." Fortunately, one girl proudly answered that her favorite food was "Sugar!" Molly asks, "Guess who's coming over for a playdate?"[110]

• While touring the United States in a Volkswagon bus, Merce Cunningham and his dancers frequently had picnics. While heading toward one picnic spot, the troupe ran into problems when a large bottle of fermented passion-fruit juice popped its cork and geysered into the air. The troupe cleaned the floor of the bus — and the bottle geysered again. On one picnic, the troupe ate on the grass in front of a Howard Johnson's. After the picnic, the troupe went inside to use the bathrooms, then drove away.[111]

• At the Grand Hotel in Venice, Robert Benchley discovered that his room was next to the kitchen, and by listening he could hear what the cooks said about the various dishes the customers were ordering. The cooks praised certain dishes, and deprecated other dishes, so Mr. Benchley was able to learn which dishes to sample and which dishes to avoid.[112]

• While Ted Shawn and his dance troupe toured Japan, they occasionally ran into language problems. Charles Weidman once wanted a glass of milk, so he got on all fours and mooed like a cow, while his friend George Steares pantomimed milking. The waitress returned with a steak.[113]

• Humorist Frank Sullivan once took a large second helping, which he couldn't finish. He remarked, "My eyes were bigger than my stomach." Then he eyed his stomach, which was becoming quite large, and added, "But my stomach's catching up with them fast."[114]

• Henny Youngman could be funny even while ordering breakfast. At a restaurant, he once ordered "burned toast, soggy eggs, cold coffee." When the waiter said, "We don't serve that here," Mr. Youngman replied, "You did yesterday."[115]

• Actor Michael Brandon became a guest on *The Tonight Show* because of his mother. She wrote Johnny Carson and asked him to put her son on *The Tonight Show* so she could see if he was eating right.[116]

Friends

• Debbie Anderson tells this story about her husband, John. He was friends with an elderly man named Mr. Daves. After Mr. Daves was widowed, he grew depressed, so John took Mr. Daves with him whenever he went fishing — and he often went fishing. Later, Mr. Daves suffered a stroke, paralyzing his right side and taking away his ability to speak and necessitating that he live in a nursing home. Again, Mr. Daves grew depressed. John got permission to frequently take Mr. Daves out of the nursing home and for a ride, but getting Mr. Daves in and out of John's truck was difficult and caused Mr. Daves pain. Therefore, John announced that he was selling his truck so he could buy a van that could handle a wheelchair. In doing this, John was giving up something he dearly prized: his truck, which his wife calls a "cowboy Cadillac." John frequently takes Mr. Daves out for a ride in his new van, and he even made a special fishing pole for Mr. Daves so that they can fish together. John's wife says, "I don't know anyone who would give up their prized possession to help a friend. I hope he can be an example for others to take a step to help those who are in need."[117]

• One of the things that Molly Ringwald most admires about very young children is their ability to easily make friends. At a playground where her daughter, Mathilda, was playing, Molly saw a young girl tap Mathilda on the shoulder and ask, "What's your name?" Mathilda told her, and asked the young girl her name, which turned to be Elle. Mathilda then said, "I like cats." Elle replied, "Me, too. Let's be friends!" And they were friends.[118]

Good Deeds

• Richard Semmler, who teaches calculus and algebra at Northern Virginia Community College, is dedicated to giving money to charity. In 2005, he reached approximately $770,000 in the total amount of charitable donations he had made since graduating from college, and he hoped to give $1 million to charity before he retired. He is able to donate so much money to charity by living simply and working additional part-time jobs so that he can give away half or more of his income. He said, "If I didn't do all of the things I was doing, I would probably have a new car every two years and I would have a huge house with a huge pool. But I would not do it that way. I want to do it this way." In 2004, Mr. Semmler made $100,000 and donated $60,000 to charity. His main employer is a beneficiary of his generosity; he has donated $355,000 to fund scholarships there. Another beneficiary of his generosity is his alma mater, Plattsburgh State University of New York, to which he has donated $200,000. Other beneficiaries of his generosity include various evangelical Christian organizations. He knows where his money goes. For example, he donated $100,000 for a Habitat for Humanity house that he helped build. He said, "Most of my dollars go to very specific projects, so I know what I'm funding. I want to see my dollars at work." By the way, his generosity started with a $25 donation to his alma mater after he graduated in 1968. He said, "That's the snowball that started rolling. As it did, it got bigger and bigger and bigger."[119]

• In 1978, the car of Catherine Ryan Hyde caught fire in a bad neighborhood in Los Angeles. Two men began running toward her, and she thought that she was about to die. But instead of killing her, the two men used a blanket to put out the fire. In part as a result of that act of kindness, she wrote a novel that she titled *Pay It Forward*, which was published in 2000 and which became a 2001 movie starring Kevin Spacey, Helen Hunt, and Haley Joel Osment. One woman who was inspired by Ms. Hyde's novel is Christina Van Blake. After Ms. Van Blake lost her job in February 2009, she became depressed. As a way to fight depression, she offered to design a room free of charge, provided that the recipient of the free design do three good deeds. In six months, she had 80 clients, and she documented 240 good deeds done by those clients. She also created a Design It Forward Web site and passed her idea on to other interior designers. Martinha Javid and Joyce Heathcote formed the Rhode Island chapter of Design It Forward. Ms. Javid said, "When you come home to a space that's beautiful, you just feel good." Ms. Heathcote added, "I think we all hope as designers that maybe this will lead to business for us, but it's not our main goal. Our main goal is to change people's perspective and have them recognize opportunities to do something for someone else."[120]

• In Buffalo, New York, Waldemar Kaminski, ran a food stand in Broadway Market for over 50 years. He invested his money in the stock market, grew rich, and without publicity gave away millions of dollars. After his death in 2006, many recipients of his charity came forward. Anne Gioia, co-founder of the Roswell Park Alliance Foundation, a medical facility to which Mr. Kaminski gave many millions of dollars, said, "He didn't want anyone to know him, but I just had to thank him. Now I think we should shout it from the rooftops." Mr. Kaminski donated $1 million for an endowed chair in pediatrics for the facility; he also donated $1 million to build a two-acre park for the campus of the facility. Ms. Gioia said, "He felt that if you died a wealthy person, you had not lived a worthwhile life." He gave to many other charities as well, and he also helped individual families with college tuition and with mortgage payments. One of his nieces, Marsha Kaminski, who lives in Oakland, CA, said, "It wasn't a handout. He was supportive and helped them maintain their dignity. If they were helping themselves, he wanted to help, too." She added, "He didn't need the material things for happiness. He enjoyed just being with people and doing what he could for them."[121]

• In February 2011, a single mother with four children cried after losing $2,500 (her income tax refund) following a trip to the Sierra Central Credit Union in Yuba City, California. Fortunately for her, some Good Samaritans saw $100 bills blowing in the wind and collected them, along with her wallet. Among the Good Samaritans were 27-year-old Yvette Carino and 32-year-old Sam Yath. Ms. Carino, an employee of the credit union, was driving when she saw money blowing in the wind. She stopped her car, and she telephoned the police. The Good Samaritans were able to recover $2,100, which Yuba City police returned to the single mother, whose name was not released. When a police officer knocked on her door, she opened it and exclaimed, "Oh, no, not more bad news!" She told the police officer that she had lost her wallet, and the police officer asked, "This wallet?"[122]

• A person who posts using the name "Mitchell" wrote on Helpothers.org, "I know that my kids have always been kind-hearted and would do whatever they could for anyone else, but when I learned about a recent act of kindness my teenage son did for a friend, it has really touched my heart." Mitchell's son would go to school with lunch money in his pocket, but he would come home hungry. Mitchell found out that his son was sharing his lunch money with a friend who never had money for lunch. Now Mitchell makes sure that the son leaves for school with lunch money for two in his pocket. Mitchell says, "The pride I carry in my heart is knowing my sons are growing up to be such fine young men and my daughter a fine young woman. The one thing we have always taught our kids, and it has carried them through their lives, is to 'start at the heart.'"[123]

• Tyrone Curry, an African-American janitor and track and field coach at Evergreen High School in Washington state, has wanted a new track for a long time: "Ten years ago, I said if I win some money, I'm going to put a track here." He did win some money in the state lottery: almost $3.4 million. He gave his school district $40,000 — which is matched with a $75,000 youth sports grant — for a brand-new track. Mr. Curry appreciates the students: "Kids do things for you. They keep you young." The students also appreciate him. Devante Botello, a senior, says, "Tyrone goes above and beyond in the sports he coaches. It's a deep feeling. All I can say is thanks."[124]

• In Hunt, Texas, a standard poodle named Leo rescued Lana Callahan's two children, 11-year-old Sean and nine-year-old Erin, from a rattlesnake they came across while playing. Leo leapt between the two children and the 5½-foot diamondback rattlesnake that bit Leo six times in the head. Leo survived, and he was named the Ken-L Ration Dog Hero of the Year for 1984.[125]

Heroes

• Fifth-grader Evan Siegel is a crossing guard and a hero. In Vancouver, Washington, he saved the life of a little girl by pulling her out of the path of a car moving quickly toward her. The driver was texting and not watching the street. Evan says, "I was like, you know, I can't let her get hit, so I had to pull her in. It really didn't matter to me at that point. I just wanted to keep her safe." Carol Stein, patrol adviser at Salmon Creek Elementary School, gives the crossing guards a week of training in how to do their jobs. She saw the near-accident: "When I saw it, I was in a position that I couldn't reach it in time, and thank goodness he was, and he acted exactly like I would have hoped." She points out, "It's a horrible crosswalk. Everyone agrees it's not a good situation, but this is how they designed it, and so we have to deal with it." She adds about Evan, "He's very responsible. He is one of the more mature fifth-graders that we've got." Because he is so responsible and mature, Ms. Stein handpicked him to work at that crosswalk. Evan takes his job seriously. He says, "A lot of kids think it's just fun and games, but it's really not when it comes to safety for these little kids and stuff." In April 2011, Evan and six other crossing-guard heroes were awarded Lifesaving Medals given by the AAA's nationwide School Safety Patrol program. AAA spokeswoman Jennifer Huebner-Davidson says, "Every year we have more than 600,000 patrolers nationwide in 31,000 schools who are volunteering their time before and after school to get kids to school safely." She adds, "Occasionally, we will have a case where a patroler has saved the life of another student [or other person] while on duty." In 1949, the AAA began awarding the Lifesaving Medal to each of these crossing-guard heroes. Evan says about his life-saving heroism, "It kind of let me feel like I was a hero, kind of, a little bit. Like Superman saving someone from the streets."[126]

• In April 2011 a 44-year-old tourist named Helen Beard, from Worksop, England, saw a one-year-old toddler dangling from the fourth-floor balcony of an Econo Lodge hotel in Orlando, Florida. She ran beneath the balcony and watched as the toddler fell, striking the third-floor balcony. Ms. Beard managed to break the fall of the toddler, who was taken to a hospital. The child's mother, 20-year-old Helena Myles, said, "I'm thanking the Lord above right now for saving my child's life. I'm also thanking that lady because she was an angel sent from heaven." She added about her daughter, Jah-Nea, "She's perfectly fine. Not a scratch on her body." Ms. Myles said that a friend had been watching Jah-Nea at the time of the fall. She said, "I'm not upset with anyone. I've had it out with my friends. But other than that, I'm thanking God right now that my child's here." Ms. Beard said that she is not a hero: "Absolutely not. I did what needed to be done. I didn't want a fuss. Anyone would have done it. I think you just act instinctively. I ran. I knew I needed to catch her. I had to do something. I guess I was hoping someone else would catch her, but I was the one who was there." Orlando authorities awarded Ms. Beard a Medal of Merit. Orange County Sheriff Jerry Demings said, "Mrs. Beard showed unusual instinct and initiative when she exited from the swimming pool area and was able to catch the child as she fell, thus saving her from extreme physical injuries and/or death."[127]

• San Quentin State Prison has convicts who are also heroes. Selected nonviolent offenders are trained to be paramedics and firefighters. They live in a firehouse outside the prison walls but are still on prison property. They respond to emergency calls, including calls from prison and from San Francisco Bay. In April 2011 the prison emergency workers succeeded in saving the life of a woman in her 40s (no name given), but unfortunately they could not save the life of 44-year-old James Laurel. The couple had been boating. Mr. Laurel tried to start the engine and fell overboard in the bay. When he tried to get back in the boat, he capsized it and it sank. The couple were in the water for approximately 90 minutes, and Mr. Laurel was not wearing a life vest. A tower guard heard a cry for help and then sent the convict emergency workers to try to save the couple. They saved the woman, but Mr. Laurel was pronounced dead at Marin General Hospital. Prisoner Derrick Edgerly dove into the water to try to save the couple. He said, "I took my turnouts [a firefighter's protective clothing] off, went over the wall and went into the Bay. There was no fear or hesitation. The guy needed help." Mr. Edgerly added, "It's an opportunity out here to show people that even though we made a mistake and we have some debt to society, we are still human beings, and we care for people and want to help people."[128]

• When mixed martial arts fighter Jon Jones and his trainers, Greg Jackson and Mike Winkeljohn, saw a theft in progress in the streets of Paterson, New Jersey, they took action. The thief was breaking into a car and taking items. The three men shouted at the thief, who started to run away. They chased him and Mr. Jones, the youngest of the three men, caught him first and tripped him. The other two men made sure that the thief was not armed. While subduing the thief, the three men used mixed martial arts techniques: foot sweep, double-leg, and arm bar. Police then arrived and arrested the suspect. Almost eight hours after chasing the burglar, Mr. Jones defeated Mauricio Rua with a third-round TKO in a mixed martial arts fight. By the way, when the three men saw the theft in progress, they were on the way to a waterfall to meditate. After subduing the thief, they made it to the waterfall. Mr. Jackson said, "It was an incredibly beautiful waterfall."[129]

• On the beach of Daytona Beach, Florida, in March 2011 a woman snatched the purse of Angela Baldwin and took off running. Angela's two children — 12-year-old Angel Baldwin and 10-year-old Carina Baldwin also took off running — after the purse-snatcher. Angel said, "I kept saying, 'Give me my mom's purse back,' and she kept saying 'I have no idea what you're talking about.'" Carina followed the woman into a woman's restroom, and the woman tossed the purse away and then ran away again. Police arrested and charged a woman with grand theft charges soon after. The two children are heroes, but their mother says, "I'm very proud of them, but I did have a stern talk with them never to do this again ... next time you call for help!" So what do Angel and Carina want to do when they grow up? They say that they want to go into law enforcement.[130]

Husbands and Wives

• Patricia Morrison played bass in bands such as The Damned, and she noticed a lot of things that most people don't notice. For example, she noticed that the lead singer of The Damned had "a good behind to look at. Being behind the singer at most of the gigs, you notice things like that." By the way, she married the lead singer: Dave Vanian. (She says it was love at first sight, but the first sight was before she became the bass player in The Damned.) The person who married them — in Las Vegas — was an Elvis impersonator.[131]

• Husband-and-wife comedy team Jerry Stiller and Anne Meara met because of an agent. Mr. Stiller was outside the agent's office waiting to be interviewed for a job when he heard a woman scream and run out of the agent's office. The woman, an attractive redhead (Ms. Meara, of course) told him that the agent had chased her around the room. Mr. Stiller says that he went into the office to confront the agent — and the agent chased *him* around the room. Neither got the job they "interviewed" for, but both got each other.[132]

• Art Linkletter was a famous daytime TV show host in the mid-20th century. On one of his shows, a woman won a mink stole, and Mr. Linkletter put it around her shoulders and then told her, "Wait until your husband sees you in this. I bet he'll say you're beautiful." The husband was then led onstage, and Mr. Linkletter saw that the man was blind. Fortunately, the husband said exactly the right thing, "You're absolutely right, Mr. Linkletter. I can see that she is beautiful."[133]

• Mark Twain enjoying swearing, a habit his wife deplored. One day, Mr. Twain cut himself shaving, and he unleased a steady stream of swear words. His wife, hoping to cure him of his bad habit, in a calm voice repeated every swear word he had shouted. Mr. Twain was unrepentant, merely remarking, "You have the words, my dear, but you don't know the tune."[134]

• Vadim Rindin, the husband of Soviet ballerina Galina Ulanova, had a good sense of humor. Before signing a contract written in English, he took off one pair of spectacles and put on another, saying, "These are German spectacles. I think I should wear my English ones for this."[135]

• Carole Lombard's second husband was William Powell. On her honeymoon, she sent this telegram to her friends: "NOTHING NEW TO REPORT."[136]

Illnesses and Injuries

• Art Linkletter was a famous daytime TV show host in the mid-20th century. He once took part in a miracle. He and his wife, Lois, were in Tahiti following a visit to their ranch in Australia when they received a telegram that his wife's mother, Peg, had suffered a stroke and was unconscious. Of course, they immediately came home, and Mr. Linkletter followed an impulse to hold his mother-in-law's hand and tell her in a voice of authority, "Peg, I know you can hear me. Lois and I have flown all the way from Australia to tell you about our sheep. Now open your eyes and say hello." Peg opened her eyes and said, "Hello, Art." Then she closed her eyes again. This time, Mr. Linkletter said, "Come on, now keep those eyes open. We love you." She opened her eyes, and this time they stayed open. Mr. Linkletter says, "It was the only miracle I ever witnessed. I was glad it was for my mother-in-law."[137]

• Dr. Rose Smart treats many injured ballet dancers. Among other things, she pushes a dancer's lumbar back into place when needed. Normally, she does this by having the injured person lie on her back and flex her legs against her. Then Dr. Smart would tell the injured person to give a push, and the lumbar would go back into place. However, early in her career, she was unaware of the strength of ballet dancers. She once told a ballerina to push her leg with all her strength — and Dr. Smart ended up peeling herself from the wall. On another occasion, she did the same procedure with a male dancer, and he broke one of her ribs. Now she uses a different procedure to treat dancers with lumbar problems.[138]

• Polly, the young niece of Alexander Woollcott, had to see a doctor because of a sore leg. Polly was convinced that she was going to die, and she accepted her fate, but her mother was terribly upset, especially when Polly talked about dying. When they arrived at the doctor's office, the doctor looked at Polly, who was serene, and he looked at Polly's mother, who was distraught. Then he stuck a thermometer into the mother's mouth.[139]

• Don Marquis suffered a series of strokes, which made him unable to work. Low on funds, he resigned from The Players Club. The treasurer of the club, David McKinley, wrote him a letter, to which Mr. Marquis responded, "My dear Dave, I have your letter in which you express the hope that Dame Fortune may be smiling on me. She is, but it is the most sarcastic goddam smile I ever saw on anyone's face."[140]

• F.E. Smith, later Lord Birkenhead, once cross-examined a boy who claimed that his arm had been crippled in an accident. He asked the boy, "Will you show me just how high you can lift your arm?" The boy raised his arm a little. F.E. then said, "Thank you, and now will you show me just how high you could lift it before the accident?" The boy then raised his arm high over his head. Case closed.[141]

• Staying in a hospital can be expensive for the patient, the insurance company, or the government, or a combination of these. When Quaker humorist Tom Mullen was in a hospital, he roomed with a Medicare patient who wanted a nurse to put this sign by his bed: "Your Tax Dollars at Work." By the way, not all nurses have a good bedside manner. When Mr. Mullen was in a hospital, a nurse looked at his medical chart and then told him, "You are one sick puppy."[142]

• British war hero Lord Nelson had one arm. A stupid person once told him, "I beg your pardon, my lord, but you have only one arm." Lord Nelson used his remaining arm to pick up his empty sleeve, then he looked into it with a surprised look on his face. "Bless my soul," he said. "I do believe you are right."[143]

• While on his deathbed, John Philpot Curran coughed frequently. When his physician told him that he was coughing with more difficulty, he replied, "That is surprising, since I have been practicing all night."[144]

Language

• Chico Marx sometimes asked his daughter, Maxine, to speak French in front of French visitors because she had studied French for years with private teachers. Charles Boyer complimented her accent, and Chico said, "She better have a good accent. It cost me $20,000." Maxine met someone through a practical joke. She and some girlfriends were thinking of someone to prank-call. One girlfriend worked as a teller in bank, and she had Maxine call a bank customer and pretend to be from France and to have met him as a party. She called him, faked a French accent, and pretended to know him. He asked her to meet him for dinner, she accepted, and all during dinner she kept up the fake French accent. She discovered that she liked him — a lot — and at the end of the dinner, she said in her fake French accent that she had something to tell him. Then, in her regular American voice, she said, "I really don't have to talk like that at all." Fortunately, he laughed. Later, they got married.[145]

• Lord Phillimore (1845-1929) once tried a man who was accused of murdering his wife. Lord Phillimore asked him, "Did you say to your wife, 'If you bloody well don't take care, you will repent of it'?" The defendant replied that he couldn't have said that because he didn't use that particular word. Lord Phillimore asked, "I suppose it is the word beginning with 'b' that you do not use." The man replied, "Oh, no! I do use that word. It's the word 'repent' which I don't use."[146]

• Ballet master George Balanchine, who was born in Russia with the name Gyorgy Balanchivadze, knew English well, but he often used Russian sentence constructions when speaking English. No problem. Those people he knew well always understood him, and he requested that when reporters quoted him, they put his sentences into correct grammatical form.[147]

• Samuel Johnson went to a market to buy fish, but he discovered that the fish at a certain shop were not fresh. The woman selling the fish argued with him and insisted that the fish were fresh, so Dr. Johnson called her a noun, an adverb, and a verb. Because the woman didn't know what those words meant, she thought that Dr. Johnson was insulting her.[148]

Media

• Writer Ben Hecht hated pomposity. When he was writing for his own newspaper, the *Chicago Literary Times*, the Moscow Art Players came to Chicago and performed, entirely in Russian, *The Brothers Karamazov*. Approximately 3,800 people in the audience listened to Russian actors speak Russian for four hours, then they gave the actors a tremendous ovation. Of the 3,800 people in the audience, Mr. Hecht figured that no more than 20 people could understand enough Russian to follow the play, and so the tremendous ovation they gave the play annoyed him. Because the *Chicago Literary Times* was his own newspaper, Mr. Hecht could do with it what he wanted, so he decided to have the review of the play translated into Russian and to print it that way. However, after the review was all set in Russian type, the printer dropped the type and it scattered all over the floor. Unfortunately, no one there knew how to read Russian and since the paper had to go to press right away, they picked up the type and put it back anyway they could, knowing that the review no longer made sense. As it turned out, the mistake didn't matter. After the paper was published, approximately 60 letters arrived, all praising the review written in Russian and saying that it was the best thing that the *Chicago Literary Times* had ever published.[149]

• The Chicago *Herald-American* once offered the prize of a summer job to the winner of a contest for high-school students who submitted news stories. The winner was a female student who sent in an article about a fire. Ray Brennan of the Chicago *Times*, however, recognized the article when it was printed — he had written it. Therefore, the *Times* printed both Mr. Brennan's article and the plagiarized article by the female student — they were identical. The *Times* also printed this note: "Ray Brennan, veteran *Times*man, today won a distinction never before accorded a Chicago newspaperman. He won the girl reporter prize from the *Herald-American*."[150]

Chapter 4: From Mishaps to Practical Jokes

Mishaps

• Makeup artist Kevyn Aucoin is one of those people who are supremely competent at what they do. He once made up model Cindy Crawford for a photo shoot (to create a *Vogue* cover) during which she would wear a pink outfit and a beige outfit. Before starting to apply her makeup, he asked which outfit she would wear first. Hearing that she would wear the pink outfit first, he made her up accordingly (her hair and makeup took two hours), knowing that he would have to change her makeup for the beige outfit. Unfortunately, the beige outfit arrived first, and Kevyn said, "Oh, I thought we were doing the other outfit first. I'll have to change a few things." *Vogue* editor Polly Mellon asked how long it would take, and Kevyn said, "Ten minutes." Polly then asked, "No. I mean how much time for a 'Kevyn Aucoin' makeup change?" Kevyn replied, "Ten minutes, Polly." Kevyn was such a perfectionist that if he had needed more than ten minutes to change Cindy's makeup, he would not have said that ten minutes was all he needed. (That Kevyn needed only ten minutes for the makeup change was a huge relief to the person who had mistakenly told him that Cindy would wear the pink outfit first.)[151]

• At one time, Chicago journalists would pretend to be police officers or other officials, either in person or on the telephone, in order to get information from crime scenes. Frequently, they would pretend to be Sgt. Francis "Jiggs" Donohue, the chief officer for the coroner's office. Chicago *Herald-Examiner* reporter Harry Romanoff once telephoned a barroom where a murder had occurred. On the phone, he said, "This is Sgt. Donohue of the coroner's office." The person who had answered the phone said, "That's funny. So is this." Sgt. Donohue had arrived at the murder scene faster than Mr. Romanoff had expected.

Once, Buddy McHugh of the Chicago *American* arrived very quickly on a murder scene (a house), identified himself as Sgt. Donohue, and told the person at the house, "If some newspaper guy shows up posing as me, give him the bum's rush." Soon after Mr. McHugh had left, the real Sgt. Donohue showed up, but the householder said, "Go peddle your papers. I'm wise to you. Sgt. Donohue's been here."[152]

• The New York City Ballet once appeared in Bologna, Italy, where they hired an orchestra that had been put together from musicians who played in local restaurants. Unfortunately, this orchestra did not know the music the New York City Ballet was performing, so choreographer George Balanchine told associate conductor Hugo Fiorato to get a machine gun and shoot them all! Although Mr. Balanchine wanted to cancel the performance, it was sold out and management convinced him to soldier on. The New York City Ballet performed to the music that was easiest to play, but even so, during "Serenade," the musical instruments stopped playing one by one. Mr. Fiorato sang the music for the dancers, and the musical instruments began to play again one by one — but the dancers onstage were laughing.[153]

• In 1948 bodybuilder Kirk Alyn starred as Superman in a low-budget serial. Once, Superman had to rescue two people from a burning building. Mr. Alyn acted in the scene, and the director said to him, "That was great, Kirk. But could we do it again without you straining so much? I mean, Superman is super strong — lifting a couple of humans should be easy." Mr. Alyn replied, "What do you expect? These people are heavy!" The director realized that he had made a mistake: "People? Oh, my goodness! I'm sorry. We forgot to get you the dummies!"[154]

• Anton Dolin and Alicia Markova toured the world, bringing ballet to everybody. Of course, mishaps occurred during touring. In Birmingham, Alabama, Ms. Markova fell flat on her back during Act II of *Giselle*, lying with her legs and her lilies pointing straight up, while she giggled at the indignity of her position. In Dallas, Texas, the stage floor was so slippery that at one point Mr. Dolan told the audience, "Ladies and gentlemen, we are doing our best and trying to stand up, but neither Miss Markova nor I nor our group are billed as The Ice Capades!"[155]

• In 1981, Leslie Woodies played Cassie during a tour of *A Chorus Line*. In Tulsa, Oklahoma, Ms. Woodies was dancing at an "audition" in the play when smoke began to fill the theater. The play was stopped, and the audience, cast, and crew went outside, where they discovered the smoke was coming from a fire up the street. Eventually, everyone went back inside and picked up the play where it had left off. The next line in the play — "Well, this audition is really interesting, isn't it?" — received an enormous response from the audience.[156]

• On 9 March 1944, Russian-born ballet dancer George Zoritch received his America citizenship papers. He managed to become a citizen even after missing this question on his exam: Who was the first American President? Mr. Zoritch had answered "Franklin Delano Roosevelt" because, after all, he was Mr. Zoritch's first American President. The examiner let the mistake go because Mr. Zoritch was young and would become better educated in the future.[157]

• Giuseppe di Stefano sang the part of Alfredo in Giuseppe Verdi's opera *La Traviata*. In the second act, he was supposed to throw some stage money into the face of the character Violetta — a deadly insult. Unfortunately, once on stage he discovered that his dresser had forgotten to put the stage money into a pocket — any pocket — of his costume. Forced to improvise, he slapped Violetta. The woman playing Violetta never forgave him.[158]

• Some glamorous, rich, and famous people had to work their way up from the bottom. Pop artist Andy Warhol lived in a cockroach-infested apartment during his early days working as a commercial artist in New York City. He once delivered some drawings to Carmel Snow, art director of *Harper's Bazaar*. As he pulled his drawings out of a paper bag in this very elegant setting, a cockroach crept out from between two of the pages.[159]

• Ballet dancer Maria Tallchief spoke her mind at times. During a rehearsal, choreographer George Balanchine was changing steps, as he was wont to do. Of course, this can make knowing what to do next very confusing. André Eglevsky turned, which was the old step, instead of lifting, which was the new step — and Ms. Tallchief fell on her face. As Mr. Eglevsky put it later, "She got up and looked back at me and was blunt."[160]

• Courtland Byrd once made a mistake. A barber, he cut the hair of a longtime customer named Murphy, and then he held up a hand mirror for Murphy to take to look at his haircut. But Murphy did not take the hand mirror, and suddenly Courtland remembered that Murphy was blind. Of course, the other barbers and the customers laughed. Courtland says, "If you make a donkey of yourself in the barber shop, they'll ride you."[161]

• Early in her career, Natalia Makarova had trouble dancing in *Swan Lake*. The character of Odile dances 32 fouettés in a row — a very difficult feat. The first time Ms. Makarova danced in *Swan Lake* she moved too much during the fouettés, finishing them in a rear wing, where the audience could not see her. According to Ms. Makarova, "It was as if I had been blown off-stage by the wind."[162]

• Dancing *Giselle* can be hazardous to your health. In Israel, at the end of Act 1 Alicia Markova performed a death fall that carried complete conviction — she knocked herself unconscious on the hard floor of the makeshift stage. Her fellow performers had to carry her offstage and pretend this was part of the ballet so the audience would not know what had happened.[163]

• When Ted Shawn met Ruth St. Denis for the first time, he was in her home, waiting for her to appear. Suddenly, he heard a clomping on the stairs, and he thought to himself, "Not even a maid should be permitted to make such a racket in this temple, in this home of a goddess." The clomper then walked up to Mr. Shawn and held out her hand — the clomper was Miss Ruth.[164]

• One of Anna Russell's aunts once gave her a hat. Ms. Russell didn't much care for the hat, but she wore it a few times because, after all, it was a present from a loved one. However, when her aunt saw her wearing the hat, she had hysterics laughing. Finally, Ms. Russell's aunt told her, "That's not a hat — it's a lavatory seat cover."[165]

• Ian Reid once conducted the opera *Carmen* at Heidelberg. Unfortunately, one night the singer playing Don José forgot his knife in the stabbing scene in which he murders Carmen, so he decided to strangle her instead. The singer playing Carmen didn't know what he was doing, so she fiercely fought him.[166]

• English entertainer Joyce Grenfell knew a man whom she described as being a "dangerous" smoker: Stephen Potter. His friends' carpets were dotted with small burn marks. In his worst disaster, he accidentally set on fire and burned a sofa.[167]

Money

• Andrew Tobias is a personal finance expert who spends a lot of time thinking about money. His significant other, Charles Nolan, was a fashion designer who spent a lot of time thinking about fashion. Charles was able to figure out the economics of fashion design — how to design something both fashionable and profitable. However, in his personal life, he made a lot of money, spent a lot of money, and wasted (chances are, this would be his choice of words) little time thinking about money. Each night, he would empty the money from his pockets into some handy place like a shopping bag. Whenever he returned home after visiting another country, he would do the same thing with the foreign money he had brought home with him. After Charles died, Andrew gathered up the foreign money — which made a 4-inch-high stack of paper bills. Andrew tells this anecdote about Charles' relationship to money: "Charles once gave a friend a pile of old magazines. A few weeks later, the friend came by to return a forgotten $5,000 that he had found tucked into one of them."[168]

• Sylvester Stallone and his pregnant wife were living in a $100-a-month apartment in Hollywood. He had written the screenplay for *Rocky* and wanted to star in the movie, but movie studios wanted someone else to star in it. Mr. Stallone was tempted to sell the movie script when he was offered $350,000 for it, although selling it meant that he would not star in the movie. He asked his wife what he should do. She asked him, "Have you ever seen $350,000?" He replied, "No, never." She then said to him, "Well, you won't miss it then." Mr. Stallone turned down the offer, and he received a much bigger financial offer and the opportunity to star in the film, which won a 1976 Best Picture Oscar.[169]

• British ballet was born in the early 1930s. Not surprisingly, it didn't pay very well. While dancing for Marie Rambert's company, Alicia Markova was told that she and the other dancers would be paid 6s 6d per performance, but Ms. Markova protested that this would just pay for the ballet shoes she would use in the performance. (Principal ballet dancers wear out one — or two — pairs of shoes per performance.) In addition, she would have to pay 4s for a taxi to get home after the performance. After her protest, Ms. Markova was paid 10s 6d per performance.[170]

• Wilson Mizner was constantly looking for a way to make money off suckers. Once, a rich young man spent the night drinking, then confessed to Mr. Mizner that he couldn't remember what he had done that night. Mr. Mizner immediately had a friend who was the night manager at an expensive restaurant draw up an itemized bill for almost $2,000, then convinced the rich young man that he had been the host of a very large, very expensive party in a private dining room at the expensive restaurant. Mr. Mizner and the night manager split the take.[171]

• Early in his quest to become a recognized artist instead of a recognized commercial artist, future Pop artist Andy Warhol searched for ideas about what he should paint and he asked many people for advice. Art consultant Muriel Latow told him, "I can give you an idea, but it's gonna cost you $50." Andy got a check ready to sign. She then told him, "What do you like most in the world? You like money. You should paint that. And you should paint something that everybody sees every day ... like cans of soup." Andy signed the check.[172]

• After the Russian Revolution, ballet dancer Nicolas Legat opened a dance studio in England. Once he needed money to pay the rent on the studio, and he decided to ask the mother of one of his pupils for a loan. After being coached on how to ask for a loan tactfully, he went to see his pupil's mother, but his command of the English language deserted him, and so he blurted out, "Geeve me feefty pounds." (He got the loan.)[173]

• Lincoln Kirstein and George Balanchine's Ballet Society was frequently short of money. Once, they needed $1,000 for a silk curtain, but this time Mr. Kirstein, who did the fundraising, couldn't get the money. Fortunately, Mr. Balanchine appeared, clutching $500 in each hand. People asked where the money had come from, but Mr. Balanchine replied only that it had not come from a bank robbery.[174]

• Scottish poet Robert Burns and a crowd of people once witnessed a sailor save a rich man from drowning. As a reward for saving his life, the rich man gave the sailor only a shilling. The crowd became angry because of the paltry reward, but Mr. Burns said, "Let him alone. The gentleman is, of course, the best judge of what his life is worth."[175]

Music

• Sometimes, male audience members would yell "Show us your tits!" at the all-female San Francisco band Frightwig. They always yelled back, "Show us your d**ks!" [No, not ducks.] Soon, they began inviting a male audience member to come on stage and strip and dance as they played the song "A Man's Gotta Do What a Man's Gotta Do."

Once, four young fans asked if they could dance on stage to the song. They danced in their underwear and then mooned everyone. Frightwig member Deanna Ashley remembers that they had FRIGHTWIG written on their butt cheeks. She says, "It was so cute."[176]

• Thea Phillips was asked by Sir Thomas Beecham to sing soprano solo in George Frideric Handel's *Messiah*. She confessed that she did not know the part, and she was afraid to attempt to sing it because the concert was only a few weeks away, but Sir Thomas convinced her to undertake the part. Later, the two met again, and Ms. Phillips was carrying the score for *Messiah* with her so she could study wherever she was. She told Sir Thomas, "It goes everywhere with me, to work, at meals, up to bed at night." Sir Thomas asked, "Then may we trust that you will have an Immaculate Conception of the part?"[177]

• Conductor André Previn has in his office a cartoon showing a music stand marked "L.A. Symphony." On the music stand is a Help Wanted Notice: "Resident Orchestra Conductor; Party Goer; Gladhander; Fundraiser; High Visibility; Some Knowledge of Music Desirable." Mr. Previn also has in his office a cartoon of a conductor standing at a podium and reading a set of instructions: "Wave the stick until the music stops, then turn around and bow."[178]

• English entertainer Joyce Grenfell knew a couple of sisters who were interested in music. Whenever they needed a housemaid or a cowman, they would advertise for a housemaid or a cowman with a particular musical talent; for example, a contralto-housemaid or a tenor-cowman. These servants formed a choir for which the sisters provided professional direction. Frequently, the choir composed of servants gave concerts.[179]

• Conductor Arturo Toscanini was having difficulty — musically and linguistically — with a star tenor in a Swedish opera house, and finally he asked a friend who spoke Swedish, "Ask that man if he knows who I am, and tell him to get the hell off the stage." The tenor listened to the two requests, then replied, "Yes and no." After hearing the translation of the tenor's reply, Mr. Toscanini laughed and went on with the rehearsal.[180]

• Jazz musician Louis Armstrong used to sing "When It's Sleepy Time Down South," although the lyrics contained such words as "mammies" and "darkies." When singing the song, Mr. Armstrong frequently either changed the offensive words or substituted "scat" (nonsense) syllables in place of them.[181]

• Some people live their life well. Asked what he was most proud of in his life, jazz saxophonist Benny Carter, who played with Charlie Parker and Fletcher Henderson, replied, "I can't think of anything I'm not proud of."[182]

• Pianist Richard Goode became famous in part by playing Beethoven's sonatas. A fan once told him, "You are Beethoven." Mr. Goode responded by leaning toward the fan, cupping his ear, and asking, "What did you say?"[183]

• In 1968, Josef Krips conducted the San Francisco Symphony in "The Star-Spangled Banner." When the song was finished, a member of the audience yelled, "Play ball!"[184]

Names

• Names in ballet are often interesting: 1) According to ballet lingo, a particularly demanding dance is called a "puff," because the dancer will huff and puff after dancing it. Of course, no matter how strenuous the role, the dancer must wait until after exiting to huff and puff. 2) A dance writer once flattered Maria Tallchief by writing, "There's only *one* Tallchief." Other, more clever people reminded the writer that Ms. Tallchief's sister, Marjorie, was also a noted ballerina. 3) In the ballet *Giselle*, two Wilis (vampires) are given prominent roles. They are named Moyna and Zulma, but American ballet companies often give them nicknames, such as Laverne and Shirley. 4) George Balanchine once joked that all ballets should be named *Swan Lake* — that way, they would be guaranteed a large and interested audience. 5) People who are intensely devoted to ballet are known as balletomanes;

people who are intensely devoted to melodic Italian opera are known as melomanes. 6) Ballet dancers need to cover their skin yet reveal the form of their body. A person who helped them do this was Jules Léotard, a French acrobat and trapeze artist who invented the body-fitting suit that bears his name.[185]

• When H. Algeranoff was dancing with Anna Pavlova in Australia, a man named Bobbie Helpman came to him for lessons. The man showed talent, and Mr. Algeranoff told him, "This is a country where they don't take easily to men dancing. I think you'd find it would be helpful if you called yourself Robert instead of Bobbie, and added a second N to your surname; it would give it a slightly foreign sound, which would be more acceptable to the general public." Mr. Helpman — make that Mr. Helpmann — took his advice, and he made the new more foreign-sounding name famous.[186]

• Names and nicknames can be interesting. When he was 15 years old, Anton Dolin studied under dance teacher Nicolas Legat, who always called him by the nickname "Piccadilly." Mr. Dolin didn't understand the meaning of the nickname until they were traveling on a bus together. When the bus passed Piccadilly Circus, Mr. Legat pointed in its direction, and Mr. Dolin saw that he was pointing at a status of Eros. By the way, opera singer Birgit Nilsson's last name came from her father, Nils. In Sweden, sometimes a child — even a girl — is given the father's first name, to which *son* is always — and *dotter* is never — added. This then becomes the child's last name.[187]

• The writers of Jackie Gleason's TV series featuring him as blowhard Ralph Kramden wanted to call the series *The Beast*, because they felt that Ralph was like an animal. However, Mr. Gleason felt that love was a major element of the show and underlay the arguments between Ralph and his wife Alice, so he insisted that it be called *The Honeymooners*.[188]

Performing

• Dancer Agnes de Mille auditioned for impresario Billy Rose early in her career. She danced for hours in different costumes and wigs, she paid the accompanist and the dresser, and her effort was immense; however, no job offer materialized after the audition. A little later, Ms. de Mille's choreography for *Rodeo* was a hit when it premiered at the Metropolitan Opera on 16 October 1942, and Mr. Rose asked about her, "Where has she been? Who discovered her? She can't have just sprung to this eminence from nowhere. She must have been somewhere. Where did she hide herself?"[189]

• The first duet ever performed by Ruth St. Denis and Ted Shawn was a North African dance which received great applause after each performance — until they danced it in Topeka, Kansas. At the end of the dance, the audience was completely silent for a long time — until a member of the audience said with feeling: "Jesus!" Afterwards, Mr. Shawn told the story of the dance's Topeka reception to Ethel Barrymore, who commented that the audience's reaction to the dance was "a very great tribute."[190]

Politics

• In 1931, Robert Benchley, Lewis Milestone, and Douglas Fairbanks were in Italy, when they decided to pay a visit on Benito Mussolini. Because Mr. Fairbanks was a huge movie star, a visit was arranged, but when they arrived at the appointed time, they were told that Mussolini could not see them for a half-hour. They replied that they were too busy to wait, and departed, leaving behind a startled bureaucrat.[191]

• Once a woman complained to Sir Winston Churchill that she didn't like either his politics or his moustache. Sir Winston replied, "Madame, you are unlikely to come into contact with either."[192]

Practical Jokes

• Russell Johnson, who played the Professor on *Gilligan's Island*, had the hardest lines to learn because so much of what he said was scientific. One day, as a practical joke, the series' producer, Sherwood

Schwartz, wrote out a half page of scientific-sounding gibberish and told Mr. Johnson to memorize it for the next day's shooting. The next day, to Mr. Schwartz's surprise, Mr. Johnson was letter-perfect in his recitation of the gibberish. (Mr. Johnson had suspected the practical joke and had stayed up half the night to learn his lines.) By the way, in 1986, Mr. Johnson was invited to speak at Park College in Missouri. He got a kick out of the posters for his lecture: Underneath a picture of his face were the words, "See a *real* Professor speak."[193]

• Gladys Cooper once wrecked a theatrical performance with a series of practical jokes. One actor lit an exploding cigar. The actresses who were supposed to eat cookies on stage were given cookies with flannel inside them. An actress who was supposed to eat an apple discovered that the apple was made of soap. Actor Gerald du Maurier witnessed these practical jokes and worried that he would be the next victim. His character was given a parcel on stage, and he thought that when he opened the parcel, something might fly out. Relieved to discover that the parcel was not booby-trapped, he sat down on a cushioned chair — which was rigged to emit a series of squeaks.[194]

• As a young man, William Schwenck Gilbert, who was later to be the librettist of *The Pirates of Penzance*, liked to give the impression that he was important in the theatrical world. A friend asked him if he could write an order for free seats at a local play, and Mr. Gilbert very happily did so. However, when the friend presented the order at the box office, he was laughed at, and later he demanded an explanation. Mr. Gilbert explained, "You asked me whether I could write you an order for the play. I replied that I could, and I did, but I never said it would be of the least use to you."[195]

• Tibor Zana was dancing in the operetta *Count of Luxembourg* when he and the other male dancers decided to play a joke on the women dancers. In the operetta, the men and women danced a waltz, with a line of men and a line of women coming toward each other, then dancing. Before the waltz, each of the men took a big bite of an onion, then at a predetermined time breathed toward their dance partners, causing quite a few heads to turn away from the smell. The stage manager fined the male dancers for the prank, but they decided the prank was worth the fine.[196]

• In the early days of Methodism, members of a congregation sometimes had fun with preachers. Jesse Lee once preached on a verse from Acts 17:6: "These that turned the world upside down have come here also." He then said that sin had turned the world upside down, and the ministry was determined to set the world right side up. The next day he discovered that in the village he had preached at, everything that could be turned upside down had been turned upside down: wagons, boats, signs, gates, etc.[197]

• Sir Thomas Beecham was a practical joker. While conducting *Façade* in 1932, he decided to play a trick with the tempo of a polka danced by ballerina Alicia Markova. At first the tempo was normal, but as the dance progressed, he speeded up the tempo faster and faster, grinning at Ms. Markova as she speeded up her dancing. Afterwards, he admitted that he has wanted to see how fast she could dance, and he complimented her on being able to keep up with his tempo.[198]

• In an episode of *The Many Loves of Dobie Gillis*, Maynard G. Krebs, played by Bob Denver, jumps into a swimming pool. The scene was scheduled to be shot in the morning, but it kept being delayed until afternoon. When he finally jumped into the swimming pool, Mr. Denver found out why. The crew had filled the pool with ice cubes and had to wait until they melted so Mr. Denver would not know how cold the water was until he jumped in.[199]

Chapter 5: From Prejudice to Work

Prejudice

• The great black dancer Bill Robinson, aka Mr. Bojangles, fought prejudice. He and his wife were on a train going from Chicago to St. Louis when they went to the dining car to eat. To avoid trouble, they usually waited until all the white people had eaten, but this time they knew that the dining car was going to be dropped off early. There was one white man still in the dining car, so they asked if he would mind if they ate in the dining car. He didn't, so they began to seat themselves at a table. The steward said, "This table is reserved," and refused to let them be seated. Mr. Bojangles was furious and pulled out a gun. The train conductor telegraphed down the line that a madman with a gun was in the dining car. Fortunately, Mr. Bojangles was friends with the police in that town and so was not arrested — also, he had gotten rid of the gun before the police showed up. In St. Louis, he made a complaint against the steward to the railroad manager, who said he would fire the steward. However, Mr. Bojangles didn't want the man to lose his job, so he said, "I'm playing at the Orpheum Theater. If he wants to come down and apologize to me, I won't force this charge against him." The steward did apologize and saved his job.[200]

• African-American jazz great Duke Ellington once received a letter from a man who suggested that he go back to Africa and take his jungle music with him. Mr. Ellington wrote back and said that he was afraid he would not be accepted in Africa because his blood and the blood of other African-Americans had become so mingled with the blood of the letter writer and other white Americans. He did say, however, that he would consider going to Europe, where he and his people were accepted.[201]

• African-American dancer/choreographer Katherine Dunham once performed in an auditorium where the white people were seated in the better seats behind the orchestra pit and the black people, including some of her friends, were seated in the balcony. After the performance, which was wildly applauded, she told the audience, "This is goodbye. I shall not appear here again until people like me can sit with people like you."[202]

• People with mental retardation are sometimes victims of prejudice. Louise Fish, who lives in Minnesota, became mentally retarded as a result of having meningitis as a baby. At school, other students sometimes hit her or pulled her hair, but she wouldn't cry until she got home. Some people, including her brother Matt, stood up for her. When people made fun of Leslie, Matt would explain why she was different.[203]

Problem-Solving

• Anna Russell was a famous singer of parodies of opera arias. During one of her early tours, she reached a low point during a lumbermen's stag night at a hotel in Chicago. The featured performers of the evening were strippers, so when Ms. Russell appeared, the lumbermen began to yell, "Take it off!" However, being a comedian, Ms. Russell responded, "I shall not take it off. I shall put it on!" Then she went from table to table, grabbing tablecloths and wrapping them around her body, and strewing broken glass behind her. She managed to leave the scene with her honor intact, but because of the bill for breakage, she made no money that night.[204]

• Bruce Lee was a master of the martial arts, but he became a master in spite of his physical limitations. One of his legs was almost one inch shorter than the other, so he developed a stance with the left foot leading. He discovered that his physical limitation gave him an advantage in certain kinds of kicks because a greater impetus came from his uneven stance. In addition, he wore contact lens because he was nearsighted and unable to see an opponent until the opponent was close. In fact, Mr. Lee began to study the martial art of wing-chun because it was ideal for up-close fighting.[205]

• What is a polite way to stop talking to someone on the telephone? Mike Desert remembers talking to Kathleen Hanna of Bikini Kill and Le Tigre. After they had talked for a while, Kathleen said, "I need to run because my bath water is running." A week later, Mike's girlfriend of the time talked to Kathleen on the telephone, and after they had talked for a while, Kathleen made the same excuse! Mike is OK with that. Now, when he needs a polite way to stop talking to someone on the telephone, he says, "I need to run because my bath water is running."[206]

• Giuseppe de Stefano was a talented opera singer, but sometimes erratic when it came to showing up to perform. Once, his wife called Sir Rudolf Bing, the general manager of the Metropolitan Opera, to say that her husband was very ill and could not sing that evening. Sir Rudolf replied that since her husband was so ill, he ought not to stay at home, and so he would send an ambulance to pick him up and take him to the hospital. Mr. Stefano made a remarkable recovery and showed up to sing.[207]

• At Ted Shawn's Jacob's Pillow, a dance retreat, was an outhouse, the inside of which was papered with covers from *The New Yorker*. This resulted in several visitors new to Jacob's Pillow staying too long in the outhouse. One woman spent too much time there, so a male dancer — in great necessity — started to urinate on the side of the outhouse. The woman flew out of the outhouse, ran straight ahead, and looked neither left nor right.[208]

• Jazz musician Louis Armstrong faced a problem after his recording of "Mack the Knife" became a huge hit. Audiences requested it, but the sheet music had been lost, so his band couldn't play it. Fortunately, he solved the problem by taking the members of his band to a place with a jukebox. He kept pouring dimes into the jukebox, and as "Mack the Knife" played over and over, members of his band wrote down the music.[209]

• Alexandre Danilova once lost her underpants while dancing the part of a rich woman in Leonide Massine's *Jardin Public*. Ms. Danilova finished her dance, but left her underpants behind when she exited the stage. Tamara Toumanova, dancing the part of a poor woman, came on stage, picked up the underpants, then flung them offstage as if they were a symbol of what her character most detested — wealth.[210]

• The music for the Merce Cunningham dance titled *Springweather and People* made heavy use of piano pedals. During a performance in California, the pedals came entirely away from the piano, so composer John Cage crawled under the piano and held the pedals in place so they could be played. According to Mr. Cage, the sound under the piano was excellent, but his arms got tired during the performance.[211]

• Clara Louise Kellogg (1842-1916) owned her own opera costumes. While performing in *La Traviata*, she discovered that the co-starring tenor had chronically dirty hands and was leaving his fingerprints on her costumes. Ms. Kellogg spoke with the offending tenor, who offered to wash his hands before performances if she bought the soap — which she did for the remaining performances.[212]

• Choreographer Paul Gerdt created a *pas de deux* for Alexandra Vinogradova and Nicolas Legat, in which Ms. Vinogradova was supposed to jump into Mr. Legat's arms. Ms. Vinogradova was afraid to try this, so Mr. Gerdt — who weighed 170 pounds — demonstrated Mr. Legat's strength by running several steps, then jumping into his arms. Mr. Legat had no difficulty in catching him.[213]

• Mme. Pandit, Ambassador from India to Great Britain, once gave a dinner party at which the cook and servants had too much to drink. Checking on the dinner, she discovered that it was only half prepared and that the cook was dead drunk and lying on the floor. Very self-assured, she simply took her guests to a Chinese restaurant.[214]

• Hugh Laing once was in the middle of a dance with Alicia Markova in *Aleko* when she fainted — she was so graceful that the faint seemed part of the dance. Mr. Laing did not stop dancing, but he gathered Ms. Markova in his arms, danced offstage and gave her to some people who could help her, then danced onstage again.[215]

Royalty and Aristocracy

• Playwright Charles MacArthur had little use for snobbishness. At a fancy dinner with members of society, Mr. MacArthur had a few drops of hollandaise sauce on the front of his shirt. The snotty Grand Duke Dimitri of Russia told him, "You have some spots on your shirt." Mr. MacArthur looked at the medals on the Grand Duke's shirt and said, "I, too, am wearing my decorations." The Grand Duke replied, "Possibly from the night before last." At that, Mr. MacArthur called for the Garcon and ordered him to bring the Grand Duke's "hat and kiddy car."[216]

• As a world-famous British ballerina, Margot Fonteyn sometimes met royalty. Once, she met 15-year-old Princess Margaret. While shaking hands, Ms. Fonteyn started to lose her balance, but Princess Margaret steadied her both "expertly and unobtrusively," causing Ms. Fonteyn to think, "They must be trained for this from childhood." Princess Margaret once told Ms. Fonteyn after a ballet gala that was televised: "I must be careful what I say about the programme while the TV cameras are running. Deaf people can often lip-read from the screen."[217]

• When King Edward VII of England fell ill of appendicitis, the entire country prayed for him. He recovered. At a thanksgiving service for the king's recovery, a Church of England canon who was capable of wit used a hymn-book that had an appendix of hymns for special occasions. The canon told the congregation, "Let us all join in singing hymn number 102, 'Peace, Blessed Peace' — in the appendix."[218]

Signs

• On 15 July 1969, singer Joan Baez' husband, David Harris, was arrested for evading the draft. As the police car drove away with her husband inside, it sported a new bumper sticker that one of her husband's friends had placed on it: "RESIST THE DRAFT."[219]

• While visiting the gardens called Kagetsu-an-Tusrumi in Tokyo, Theodore Stier, who was Anna Pavlova's music director, was amused to see a large sign which stated: "NO CHEEK-TO-CHEEK DANCING. NO SHIMMYING OR SHAKING."[220]

• Signs can be misleading. A sign once said, "Ornette Coleman — Free Jazz Concert." Fans were shocked that they had to pay to attend the concert — "Free Jazz" was the name of the kind of jazz music that Mr. Coleman was playing.[221]

Sports

• Babe Zaharias was a female professional athlete when few female professional athletes existed. She won Olympic gold medals in track and field and started the Ladies Professional Golf Association (LPGA), but she played (and often excelled in) many other sports. A reporter once asked her if there was anything she did not play. She replied, "Yeah. Dolls." Lots of people thought that playing sports was a masculine trait, and a woman once asked her, "Where are your whiskers?" Babe replied, "I'm sitting on them, sister, just like you."[222]

• People with mental retardation like having fun and participating in sports, too. Leslie Fish, who became mentally retarded after suffering from meningitis as a baby, lives in Minnesota where winter sports are popular. She enjoys both skiing and ice skating. She and her Special Olympics team once skated at the United States National Figure Skating Championships. When she was young, she and her father sometimes pretended to smoke cigars just for fun.[223]

Travel

• Travelers sometimes have interesting experiences. While traveling in Mexico, Anna Pavlova's dance troupe ran into a problem. The proprietor of a hotel showed them a large room where he expected all the members of the troupe — male and female — to sleep. He explained that the large room was "for the family." Ms. Pavlova and her troupe found different lodgings. While Ms. Pavlova was touring in South Africa, a male Kaffir dancer named Brandy was told that she was the greatest dancer in the world. He replied, "She hasn't seen me yet."[224]

• Anna Pavlova believed in getting all she could from her travels. For example, she studied the national dances of the countries she performed in: While touring in a country for an extended time, she sought the best teachers for her dance company, so they could learn the national dances and perform them the next time they visited that country. In addition, she once spent an entire night watching the Taj Mahal under a full moon.[225]

• Early aviator Katherine Stinson was known for keeping her airplane very clean. Was this because of a woman's stereotypical concern with cleanliness? No. She explained, "It's all right if your automobile goes wrong while you are driving it. You can get out ... and tinker with it. But if your airplane breaks down, you can't sit on a convenient cloud and tinker with *that*!"[226]

• Ballerina Illaria Obidenna Ladré danced all over the world. She remembers the smells of South America vividly. Arriving at 3 a.m. in a small town, she and the dance troupe smelled freshly baked bread — quite a contrast to the smell of the town where people at a hotel dumped the contents of their chamber pots from the hotel balcony.[227]

• Sir Harry Lauder, a Scotsman, performed in Chicago, where he asked an elderly woman in the audience to come up on stage with him. She did, saying that she had come 30 miles to see him. Sir Harry replied, "But that's nothing, my dear lassie. I've just traveled 5,000 miles to see you."[228]

• When Harry Hershfield first went to Paris as an old man, he told a friend that he wished he had seen Paris 30 years earlier. The friend asked, "You mean when Paris was Paris?" "No," he said, "when Hershfield was Hershfield."[229]

• Traveler Peg Bracken likes to keep an eye on the graffiti of any country she visits. On the sea wall of Saint-Tropez, she saw this graffito: "Revolution is coming; keep your eyes on the rich men's yachts."[230]

Valentine's Day

• Toni Dukes, an African-American, is a 911 dispatcher in San Francisco who uses her own money to give gifts to homeless and other needy people. In zip-lock bags she places a hat and gloves and a package of Kleenex. On the outside she writes in black marker "From the Heart." She carries around many zip-lock bags containing gifts so that she can fulfill requests. She then will ask a needy person if he or she wants a gift, and if the answer is yes, she asks the person his or her size and favorite color. She does this a few times a month, and she notes that often the people are as grateful to have someone to talk to for a few minutes as they are to receive the gifts, hundreds of which she has given away. Near Valentine's Day in 2008, she saw a woman and said to her, "Hello, ma'am. Would you like a pair of gloves and a hat?" The woman asked, "Free?" Ms. Dukes replied, "From the heart — it's a Valentine's present."[231]

War

• The United States military forces have sometimes worried about gay and lesbian personnel. (Many gays and lesbians are patriotic and want to perform military service for their country.) For example, during World War II, General Dwight D. Eisenhower worried about lesbians in the war effort. He ordered Sergeant Johnnie Phelps to find out which members of the Women's Army Corps under his command were lesbians. She replied, "I will be happy to do this investigation .... But, sir, it would be unfair of me not to tell you, my name is going to head the list .... You should also be aware that you're going to have to replace all the file clerks, the section heads, most of the commanders, and all of the motor pool." General Eisenhower thought for a moment and then said, "Forget the order."[232]

• During World War I, Charles MacArthur, who was later a famous playwright and screenwriter, was forced to suddenly take refuge from the explosions of enemy bombs. Unfortunately, he had the bad luck to dive headfirst into an abandoned German latrine. Still, he was optimistic, thinking to himself, "MacArthur, this is the lowest point of your life. From here on everything has got to be an improvement."[233]

• Richard Wagner has the reputation of being an anti-Semite and an advocate of the Aryan race — Adolf Hitler regularly listened to Wagner's operas at Bayreuth. For these reasons, after liberating Bayreuth in World War II, African-American GIs donned opera costumes and paraded down the streets dressed as such Aryan heroes as Wotan, Siegfried, and Parsifal.[234]

• The characters in the TV series *M*A*S*H* sometimes showed inventive problem-solving. In one episode, a hawkish general who sends many young men needlessly to their deaths is stopped — the M*A*S*H surgeons fake a medical emergency and give him an unnecessary appendectomy.[235]

• General Joe Wheeler had fought for the Confederates during the Civil War. Years later, he was fighting in the Spanish-American War at Las Guasimas. In the heat of battle, he forgot where he was and yelled, "Come on, boys, we've got the damn Yankees on the run!"[236]

Wit

• Bob Denver appeared in the movie *Back to the Beach*, starring Frank Avalon and Annette Funicello. In it, he played a bartender who looked very much like Gilligan (Mr. Denver played Gilligan on the TV series *Gilligan's Island*). In the movie, his character said that he once knew a guy who could build a nuclear reactor out of coconuts and pineapples, but the guy didn't know how to build a boat.[237]

• Fred Astaire danced in many movies with Ginger Rogers. When Ms. Rogers won the Oscar for her role in *Kitty Foyle*, Mr. Astaire sent her a very short telegram: "Ouch." By the way, Mr. Astaire had a pet cockatiel that he named Gregory — after a famous movie star — because it pecked.[238]

• Charles Talleyrand once was riding in a carriage with a bore who talked incessantly. Another carriage drew up beside them — inside it a man could be seen giving a huge yawn. Taking advantage of the situation, Mr. Talleyrand told his boring companion, "Hush — you are overheard."[239]

• Opera singer Eileen Farrell was a large woman with a sense of humor. She once joked, "They're shipping my costume in a boxcar."[240]

Work

• Fred Astaire was a hard worker who believed in practicing even things that weren't likely to appear in his movies. While rehearsing for *Funny Face*, he was dancing with an umbrella, and director Stanley Donen asked him to open the umbrella and dance with it to see if any moves happened that would look good in the movie. Mr. Astaire opened the umbrella, danced with it, then closed it again — all impeccably. Mr. Donen asked him how he was able to do that so well, and Mr. Astaire replied, "I've practiced it." According to Mr. Donen, that was part of the secret of Mr. Astaire's success: "He would practice things that didn't have any immediate connection with anything." Mr. Astaire often kept on dancing during pauses in the shooting of his films. Co-star Leslie Caron remembers going out for some air, then returning back to the studio to see Mr. Astaire dancing with a coat hanger.[241]

• The Hasidim loved Israel. Rabbi Velvele of Zbaraz moved to *Eretz Israel*, but money was hard to come by and so his wife became a washerwoman in order for her and her husband to avoid taking money from charity to live. Rabbi Yaakov Shimshon of Sheptivka came to visit and he saw the rabbi's wife washing laundry in the yard. Believing that the rabbi's wife would feel humiliated if she knew that he had seen her washing her laundry, he attempted to leave quietly without being seen. However, the rabbi's wife saw him. She knew why he had attempted to leave before revealing his presence, so she said to him, "Do not be concerned, Rabbi. This is not my personal wash, but rather work that I undertake, and which ensures our livelihood. Thank God that we are able to live in *Eretz Israel* and to live off our manual labor."[242]

• Rudolf Bing knew a man called Childs, whom he described as the "perfect butler." Childs was a butler to John Christie, and he also helped to take care of Mr. Christie's guests. He knew Mr. Bing liked to sleep later than the other guests and skip breakfast, and one morning he woke Mr. Bing with the announcement, "Breakfast at eight-thirty, sir." Mr. Bing then asked him the time, and Childs replied, "Nine o'clock, sir." Once, Mr. Bing asked where Mr. Christie was, and Childs told him — it was a place that surprised Mr. Bing. He asked Childs, "How do you know he is *there*? Did you ask him before he left?" Childs replied, "A good butler never asks his master where he is going, but he always knows."[243]

• Fred Astaire used the phrase "a good deed" to refer to a good step in his dancing. Sometimes he would worry that he had not accomplished much while working on a dance, so he would call co-choreographer Hermes Pan and ask, "Did we get a good deed today?" Frequently, Mr. Pan was able to reassure him and mention a certain step that they had worked out together. Fred Astaire once gave Mr. Pan one of his shoes and a note that said, "To Pan, in memory of those thousands of rotten hours in rotten rehearsal halls." Mr. Astaire was sensitive to language and refused to say certain lines in his movies. For example, a script called for him to say, "My feet hurt." Mr. Astaire read the script, saw the line, and said, "I won't say it. I would never say it. My feet hurt? Never."[244]

• Albert E. Kahn spent several months photographing Soviet ballerina Galina Ulanova, always being careful not to interrupt her in her practices, performances, or teaching sessions. Once, he did interrupt. Ms. Ulanova had been teaching 19-year-old Katya Maximova to dance *Giselle*, and at one point she had embraced her.

Mr. Kahn had not caught the moment with his camera, so he asked her to repeat the embrace, saying, "It was such a beautiful moment." She replied, "That beautiful moment is gone forever. Now you mustn't interrupt us. We're working."[245]

• Country music singer Willie Nelson used to work at Texas Power and Light Company trimming tree branches away from around high line wires. One day he tried sliding down a rope to the ground, but his hand got caught in the rope. Because the pain was unbearable and he felt as if he were losing his fingers, he ordered his partner to cut the rope and let him drop to the ground, hoping that he would fall between the wires and not on one. Luckily, he fell exactly between the wires. He then picked himself up, walked off the job, and never returned.[246]

• Oscar Wilde once worked for a women's magazine, *The Lady's World*. After reviewing the magazine, he convinced its publisher to change its name to *The Woman's World* and he changed its content from only what women wear to more of what women think and feel. After a couple of years, he left the magazine. Shortly before leaving, he was asked how much time he spent working at the magazine. Mr. Wilde replied, "I used to go three times a week for an hour a day, but I have since struck off one of the days."[247]

• Sometimes set designers want scenes that are impossible to build. Carpenter Frank Kirby tells of a designer who wanted a piece suspended over the stage. His model had the piece suspended by a wire, but he said he didn't want the piece suspended by a wire because the audience could see it. Mr. Kirby told him, "You do it. When you can get it to stay up on the model without any support, we'll get it to stay up on the stage."[248]

• Suzanne Farrell and her male partner were having technical difficulties during a choreography session with George Balanchine. Correcting the technical difficulties took precious time, so Ms. Farrell telephoned Mr. Balanchine to apologize: "Oh, George, I'm so sorry that you have to work so hard to make us look good." He replied,

"Don't worry, dear. I have to work hard to make everybody look good."[249]

• James McNeill Whistler, the famous painter, held several jobs early in his career, at which he was always late — in the opinion of his co-workers. Mr. Whistler's opinion was different: "I was not too late; the office opened too early."[250]

Appendix A: Book Bibliography

Adler, Bill. *Jewish Wit and Wisdom*. New York: Dell Publishing Co., Inc, 1969.

Algeranoff, H. *My Years With Pavlova*. London: William Heinemann Ltd., 1957.

Anecdotes of the Hour By Famous Men. New York: Hearst's International Library Company, 1914.

Atkinson, Margaret F. and May Hillman. *Dancers of the Ballet*. New York: Alfred A. Knopf, 1955.

Aucoin, Kevyn. *The Art of Makeup*. New York: HarperCollins*Publishers*, 1996.

Beach, Scott. *Musicdotes*. Berkeley, CA: Ten Speed Press, 1977.

Benchley, Nathaniel. *Robert Benchley*. New York: McGraw-Hill Book Company, Inc., 1955.

Bing, Sir Rudolf. *5000 Nights at the Opera*. Garden City, NY: Doubleday and Company, Inc., 1972.

Bland, Alexander. *Fonteyn and Nureyev*. New York: Times Books, 1979.

Blum, David. *Quintet: Five Journeys Toward Musical Fulfillment*. Ithaca and London: Cornell University Press, 1999.

Boxer, Tim. *The Jewish Celebrity Hall of Fame*. New York: Shapolsky Publishers, 1987.

Bracken, Peg. *But I Wouldn't Have Missed It for the World!* New York: Harcourt Brace Jovanovich, Inc., 1973.

Brady, Logan Munger. *Amusing Anecdotes: Humorous Stories With a Moral*. Ann Arbor, MI: Ann Arbor Book Company, 1993.

Brandreth, Gyles. *Great Theatrical Disasters*. New York: St. Martin's Press, 1982.

Bredeson, Carmen. *Ruth Bader Ginsburg: Supreme Court Justice*. Springfield, NJ: Enslow Publications, Inc., 1995.

Brown, Michèle and Ann O'Connor. *Hammer and Tongues: A Dictionary of Women's Wit and Humour*. London: J.M. Dent and Sons, Ltd., 1986.

Bryan III, J. *Merry Gentlemen (and One Lady)*. New York: Atheneum, 1985.

Burden, Zora von, editor. *Women of the Underground: Music*. San Francisco, CA: Manic D Press, 2010.

Burke, John. *Rogue's Progress: The Fabulous Adventures of Wilson Mizner*. New York: G.P. Putnam's Sons, 1975.

Carle, Eric. *Flora and Tiger: 19 Very Short Stories from My Life*. New York: Philomel Books, 1997.

Chan, Luke. *101 Lessons of Tao*. Cincinnati, OH: Benefactor Books, 1995.

Danilova, Alexandra. *Choura: The Memoirs of Alexandra Danilova*. New York: Alfred A. Knopf, 1986.

de Mille, Agnes. *Portrait Gallery*. Boston, MA: Houghton Mifflin Company, 1990.

Deffaw, Chip. *Jazz Veterans: A Portrait Gallery*. Photographs by Nancy Miller Elliott and John & Andreas Johnsen. Fort Bragg, CA: Cypress House Press, 1996.

Denver, Bob. *Gilligan, Maynard and Me*. New York: Carol Publishing Group, 1993.

Dolin, Anton. *Alicia Markova: Her Life and Art*. New York: Hermitage House, 1953.

Drucker, Hal, and Sid Lerner. *From the Desk Of*. Photographs by Sing-Si Schwartz. San Diego: Harcourt Brace Jovanovich, Publishers, 1989.

Farrell, Suzanne. *Holding On to the Air*. New York: Summit Books, 1990.

Fonteyn, Margot. *Autobiography*. New York: Alfred A. Knopf, 1976.

Ford, Corey. *The Time of Laughter*. Boston, MA: Little, Brown and Company, 1967.

Fountain, Richard, compiler. *The Wit of the Wig*. London: Leslie Frewin Publishers, Limited, 1968.

Fox, Grace. *Everyday Etiquette*. Garden City, NY: Doubleday Direct, Inc., 1996.

Frank, Rusty E. *Tap! The Greatest Tap Dance Stars and Their Stories, 1900-1955*. New York: William Morrow and Company, Inc., 1990.

Franks, A.H., editor. *Pavlova: A Collection of Memoirs*. New York: Da Capo Press, Inc., 1956.

Giles, Sarah. *Fred Astaire: His Friends Talk*. New York: Doubleday, 1988.

Goodman, Jack, and Albert Rice. *I Wish I'd Said That!* New York: Simon and Schuster, 1935.

Greenberg, Jan, and Sandra Jordan. *Andy Warhol: Prince of Pop*. New York: Delacorte Press, 2004.

Gregory, John, editor. *Heritage of a Ballet Master: Nicolas Legat*. London: Dance Books, Ltd., 1978.

Grenfell, Joyce. *Joyce Grenfell Requests the Pleasure*. London: Macdonald Futura Publishers Ltd., 1976.

Greskovic, Robert. *Ballet 101*. New York: Hyperion, 1998.

Gruen, John. *People Who Dance*. Pennington, NJ: Princeton Book Company, 1988.

Guerilla Girls. *Bitches, Bimbos and Ballbreakers: The Guerilla Girls' Illustrated Guide to Female Stereotypes*. New York: Penguin Books, 2003.

Halliwell, Leslie. *The Filmgoer's Book of Quotes*. New Rochelle, NY: Arlington House Publishers, 1973.

Harris, Nick. *I Wish I'd Said That!* London: Octopus Books Limited, 1984.

Haskins, Jim, and N.R. Mitgang. *Mr. Bojangles: The Story of Bill Robinson*. New York: William Morrow and Company, Inc., 1988.

Hecht, Ben. *Charlie: The Improbable Life and Times of Charles MacArthur*. New York: Harper & Brothers, Publishers, 1957.

Henry, Lewis C. *Humorous Anecdotes About Famous People*. Garden City, NY: Halcyon House, 1948.

Holland, Merlin. *The Wilde Album*. New York: Henry Holt and Company, 1997.

Holloway, Stanley. *Wiv a Little Bit O' Luck*. As told to Dick Richards. New York: Stein and Day, Publishers, 1967.

Hope, Bob. With Bob Thomas. *The Road to Hollywood: My Forty-Year Love Affair With the Movies*. Garden City, NY: Doubleday & Company, Inc., 1977.

Hurok, S. *S. Hurok Presents: A Memoir of the Dance World*. New York: Hermitage House, 1953.

Hyams, Joe. *Zen in the Martial Arts*. New York: Bantam Books, 1979.

Irving, Gordon, compiler. *The Wit of the Scots*. London: Leslie Frewin Publishers, Inc., 1969.

Javna, John. *The Best of TV Sitcoms*. New York: Harmony Books, 1988.

Jessel, George. *Jessel, Anyone?* Englewood Cliffs, NJ: Prentice-Hall, Inc., 1960.

Johnson, Russell, and Steve Cox. *Here on Gilligan's Isle*. New York: HarperCollins Publishers, Inc., 1993.

Jones, Peter C., and Lisa MacDonald. *Hero Dogs: 100 True Stories of Daring Deeds*. Kansas City, MO: Andrews McMeel, 1997.

Kahn, Albert E. *Days With Ulanova*. New York: Simon and Schuster, 1962.

Karkar, Jack and Waltraud, compilers and editors. *... And They Danced On*. Wausau, WI: Aardvark Enterprises, 1989.

Kenefick, Colleen, and Amy Y. Young, compilers and editors. *The Best of Nursing Humor*. Philadelphia, PA: Hanley & Belfus, Inc., 1993.

Klosty, James, editor and photographer. *Merce Cunningham*. New York: Saturday Review Press/E.P. Dutton and Co., Inc, 1975.

Kristy, Davida. *George Balanchine: American Ballet Master*. Minneapolis, MN: Lerner Publications Company, 1996.

Ladré, Illaria Obidenna. *Illaria Obidenna Ladré: Memoirs of a Child of Theatre Street*. With Nancy Whyte. Seattle, WA: The Author, 1988.

Legat, Nicolas. *Ballet Russe: Memoirs of Nicolas Legat*. Translated by Sir Paul Dukes. London: Methuen & Co., Ltd., 1939.

Linkletter, Art. *Women are My Favorite People*. Garden City, NY: Doubleday & Company, Inc., 1974.

Lyman, Darryl. *The Jewish Comedy Catalog*. Middle Village, NY: Jonathan David Publishers, Inc., 1989.

Marberry, Craig. *Cuttin' Up: Wit and Wisdom from Black Barber Shops*. New York: Doubleday, 2005.

Marcus, Leonard S., compiler and editor. *Funny Business: Conversations with Writers of Comedy*. Somerset, MA: Candlewick Press, 2009.

Makarova, Natalia. *A Dance Autobiography*. Edited by Gennady Smakov. New York: Alfred A Knopf, Inc., 1979.

Markova, Alicia. *Giselle and Me*. New York: The Vanguard Press, Inc., 1960.

Markova, Alicia. *Markova Remembers*. Boston, MA: Little, Brown and Company, 1986.

Marx, Groucho. *The Secret Word is Groucho*. With Hector Arce. New York: G.P. Putnam's Sons, 1976.

Marx, Maxine. *Growing Up with Chico*. New York: Limelight Editions, 1986.

Maser, Frederick E., and Robert Drew Simpson. *If Saddlebags Could Talk: Methodist Stories and Anecdotes*. Franklin, TN: Providence House Publishers, 1998.

McNey, Martha. *Leslie's Story*. Minneapolis, MN: Lerner Publications Company, 1996.

McPhaul, John J. *Deadlines and Monkeyshines: The Fabled World of Chicago Journalism*. Englewood Cliffs, NJ: Prentice-Hall, Inc. 1962.

Monem, Nadine, editor. *Riot Grrrl: Revolution Girl Style Now!* London: Black Dog Publishing, 2007.

Montague, Sarah. *Pas de Deux: Great Partnerships in Dance*. New York: Universe Books, 1981.

Mullen, Tom. *Living Longer and Other Sobering Possibilities*. Richmond IN: Friends United Press, 1996.

Neale, Wendy. *Ballet Life Behind the Scenes*. New York: Crown Publishers, Inc., 1982.

Nelson, Willie. *The Facts of Life and Other Dirty Jokes*. New York: Random House Trade Paperback, 2003.

Newman, Barbara and Leslie E. Spatt. *Swan Lake*. London: Dance Books, 1983.

O'Connell, Charles. *The Other Side of the Record*. New York: Alfred A. Knopf, 1949.

Old, Wendie C. *Duke Ellington: Giant of Jazz*. Springfield, NJ: Enslow Publications, Inc., 1996.

Old, Wendie C. *Louis Armstrong: King of Jazz*. Springfield, NJ: Enslow Publications, Inc., 1998.

Orgill, Roxane. *Shout, Sister, Shout!* New York: Margaret K. McElderry Books, 2001.

Patelson, Alice. *Portrait of a Dancer, Memories of Balanchine: An Autobiography*. New York: Vantage Press, 1995.

Pearson, Hesketh. *Lives of the Wits*. New York: Harper & Row, Publishers, 1962.

Procter-Gregg, Humphrey. *Beecham Remembered*. London: Gerald Duckworth & Company Limited, 1976.

Primack, Ben, adapter and editor. *The Ben Hecht Show: Impolitic Observations from the Freest Thinker of 1950s Television*. Jefferson, NC: McFarland & Company, Inc., Publishers, 1993.

Rappel, Yoel. *Yearning for the Holy Land: Hasidic Tales of Israel*. Translated by Shmuel Himmelstein. New York: Adama Books, 1986.

Ringwald, Molly. *Getting the Pretty Back: Friendship, Family, and Finding the Perfect Lipstick*. New York: HarperCollins Publishers, 2010.

Rosten, Leo. *People I Have Loved, Known or Admired*. New York: McGraw-Hill Book Company, 1970.

Russell, Anna. *I'm Not Making This Up, You Know: The Autobiography of the Queen of Musical Parody*. New York: The Continuum Publishing Company, 1985.

Rutkowska, Wanda. *Famous People in Anecdotes*. Warszawa: Wydawnictwa Szkolne i Pedagogiczne, 1977.

Schochet, Stephen. *Hollywood Stories: Short, Entertaining Anecdotes About the Stars and Legends of the Movies!* Los Angeles, CA: Hollywood Stories Publishing, 2010.

Shydner, Ritch, and Mark Schiff, compilers. *I Killed: True Stories of the Road from America's Top Comics*. New York: Crown Publishers, 2006.

Slezak, Leo. *Song of Motley*. New York: Arno Press, 1977.

Steiger, Brad, and Sherry Hansen Steiger. *Animal Miracles: Inspirational and Heroic True Stories*. Holbrook, MA: Adams Media Corporation, 1999.

Stier, Theodore. *With Pavlova Around the World*. London: Hurst & Blackett, Ltd., 1927.

Story, Rosalyn M. *And So I Sing: African-American Divas of Opera and Concert*. New York: Warner Books, 1990.

Sullivan, George. *Trapped*. New York: Scholastic Inc., 1998.

Terry, Walter. *Ted Shawn: Father of American Dance*. New York: The Dial Press, 1976.

Thomas, Danny. *Make Room for Danny*. With Bill Davidson. New York: G.P. Putnam's Sons, 1991.

Thomas, Marlo. *Growing Up Laughing: My Story and the Story of Funny*. Waterville, ME: Thorndike Press, 2010. Large Print.

Vickers, Hugh. *Even Greater Operatic Disasters*. New York: St. Martin's Press, 1982.

Voss, Frederick S. *Women of Our Time: An Album of Twentieth-Century Portraits*. London: Merrell in association with the National Portrait Gallery, Smithsonian Institution, 2002.

Wagner, Alan. *Prima Donnas and Other Wild Beasts*. Larchmont, NY: Argonaut Books, 1961.

Woollcott, Barbara. *None But a Mule*. New York: The Viking Press, 1944.

Yearwood, Trisha. *Georgia Cooking in an Oklahoma Kitchen*. With Gwen Yearwood and Beth Yearwood Bernard. New York: Clarkson Potter/Publishers, 2008.

Zoritch, George. *Ballet Mystique: Behind the Glamour of the Ballet Russe*. Mountain View, CA: Cynara Editions, 2000.

Appendix B: About the Author

It was a dark and stormy night. Suddenly a cry rang out, and on a hot summer night in 1954, Josephine, wife of Carl Bruce, gave birth to a boy — me. Unfortunately, this young married couple allowed Reuben Saturday, Josephine's brother, to name their first-born. Reuben, aka "The Joker," decided that Bruce was a nice name, so he decided to name me Bruce Bruce. I have gone by my middle name — David — ever since.

Being named Bruce David Bruce hasn't been all bad. Bank tellers remember me very quickly, so I don't often have to show an ID. It can be fun in charades, also. When I was a counselor as a teenager at Camp Echoing Hills in Warsaw, Ohio, a fellow counselor gave the signs for "sounds like" and "two words," then she pointed to a bruise on her leg twice. Bruise Bruise? Oh yeah, Bruce Bruce is the answer!

Uncle Reuben, by the way, gave me a haircut when I was in kindergarten. He cut my hair short and shaved a small bald spot on the back of my head. My mother wouldn't let me go to school until the bald spot grew out again.

Of all my brothers and sisters (six in all), I am the only transplant to Athens, Ohio. I was born in Newark, Ohio, and have lived all around Southeastern Ohio. However, I moved to Athens to go to Ohio University and have never left.

At Ohio U, I never could make up my mind whether to major in English or Philosophy, so I got a bachelor's degree with a double major in both areas, then I added a Master of Arts degree in English and a Master of Arts degree in Philosophy. Yes, I have my MAMA degree.

Currently, and for a long time to come (I eat fruits and veggies), I am spending my retirement writing books such as *Nadia Comaneci: Perfect 10*, *The Funniest People in Comedy*, *Homer's* Iliad: *A Retelling in Prose*, and *William Shakespeare's* Hamlet: *A Retelling in Prose*.

By the way, my sister Brenda Kennedy writes romances such as *A New Beginning* and *Shattered Dreams*.

Appendix C: Some Books by David Bruce

Anecdote Collections

250 Anecdotes About Opera
250 Anecdotes About Religion
250 Anecdotes About Religion: Volume 2
250 Music Anecdotes
Be a Work of Art: 250 Anecdotes and Stories
The Coolest People in Art: 250 Anecdotes
The Coolest People in the Arts: 250 Anecdotes
The Coolest People in Books: 250 Anecdotes
The Coolest People in Comedy: 250 Anecdotes
Create, Then Take a Break: 250 Anecdotes
Don't Fear the Reaper: 250 Anecdotes
The Funniest People in Art: 250 Anecdotes
The Funniest People in Books: 250 Anecdotes
The Funniest People in Books, Volume 2: 250 Anecdotes
The Funniest People in Books, Volume 3: 250 Anecdotes
The Funniest People in Comedy: 250 Anecdotes
The Funniest People in Dance: 250 Anecdotes
The Funniest People in Families: 250 Anecdotes
The Funniest People in Families, Volume 2: 250 Anecdotes
The Funniest People in Families, Volume 3: 250 Anecdotes
The Funniest People in Families, Volume 4: 250 Anecdotes
The Funniest People in Families, Volume 5: 250 Anecdotes
The Funniest People in Families, Volume 6: 250 Anecdotes
The Funniest People in Movies: 250 Anecdotes
The Funniest People in Music: 250 Anecdotes
The Funniest People in Music, Volume 2: 250 Anecdotes
The Funniest People in Music, Volume 3: 250 Anecdotes
The Funniest People in Neighborhoods: 250 Anecdotes
The Funniest People in Relationships: 250 Anecdotes
The Funniest People in Sports: 250 Anecdotes
The Funniest People in Sports, Volume 2: 250 Anecdotes
The Funniest People in Television and Radio: 250 Anecdotes
The Funniest People in Theater: 250 Anecdotes

[1] Source: Karin Johnson, "Family Finds Letters From 6-Year-Old After Cancer Claims Her Proceeds From Book To Go Toward Cancer Research." WLWT.com. 10 December 2008 <http://www.wlwt.com/health/18248330/detail.html>. Also: "Girl's 'Notes Left Behind' Made Into Book: Elena Desserich Left Parents Notes Before She Died." WLWT.com. 28 October 2009 <http://www.wlwt.com/family/21429609/detail.html>. Also: "Young Artist Loses Fight With Rare Brain Cancer." WLWT.com. 13 August 2007 <http://www.wlwt.com/news/13882934/detail.html>.

[2] Source: Paul Krugman, "Wisconsin Power Play." *New York Times*. 20 February 2011 <http://www.nytimes.com/2011/02/21/opinion/21krugman.html?_r=1&ref=paulkrugman>. Also: Ian's Pizza by the Slice. Facebook. <http://www.facebook.com/pages/Ians-Pizza-by-the-Slice/72866932924?v=wall>. Accessed on 22 February 2011.

[3] Source: Suzy Corrigan, "Art, Politics and How One Grrrl Joined the Feminist Riot," pp. 154-156, 158. Collected in this book: Nadine Monem, editor. *Riot Grrrl: Revolution Girl Style Now!*

[4] Source: Roxane Orgill, *Shout, Sister, Shout!*, pp. 77-78.

[5] Source: Red Chidgey, "Riot Grrrl Writing," p. 101. Collected in this book: Nadine Monem, editor. *Riot Grrrl: Revolution Girl Style Now!*

[6] Source: Leslie Halliwell, *The Filmgoer's Book of Quotes*, pp. 47-48.

[7] Source: Darryl Lyman, *The Jewish Comedy Catalog*, p. 142.

[8] Source: Stanley Holloway, *Wiv a Little Bit O' Luck*, pp. 210-211.

[9] Source: Leslie Halliwell, *The Filmgoer's Book of Quotes*, p. 15.

[10] Source: Bob Hope, *The Road to Hollywood*, p. 91.

[11] Source: Marlo Thomas, *Growing Up Laughing: My Story and the Story of Funny*, pp. 21-22.

[12] Source: Hal Drucker and Sid Lerner, *From the Desk Of*, p. 18.

[13] Source: Rosalyn M. Story, *And So I Sing: African-American Divas of Opera and Concert*, p. 88.

[14] Source: David J. Pollay, "The Law of the Garbage Truck™." Copyright 2004 –2009. <http://davidjpollay.typepad.com/david_j_pollay/lawofthegarbagetruck.html>. Accessed on 23 March 2011.

[15] Source: Luke Chan, *101 Lessons of Tao*, p. 63.

[16] Source: Craig Marberry, *Cuttin' Up: Wit and Wisdom from Black Barber Shops*, pp. 132-133.

[17] Source: Yoel Rappel, *Yearning for the Holy Land: Hasidic Tales of Israel*, pp. 142, 146.

[18] Source: Barbara Woollcott, *None But a Mule*, pp. 107.

[19] Source: Leo Slezak, *Song of Motley*, p. 177.

[20] Source: Gyles Brandreth, *Great Theatrical Disasters*, p. 69.

[21] Source: Peg Bracken, *But I Wouldn't Have Missed It for the World!*, p. 196.

[22] Source: Gordon Irving, compiler, *The Wit of the Scots*, pp. 58-59.

[23] Source: Brad and Sherry Hansen Steiger, *Animal Miracles: Inspirational and Heroic True Stories*, pp. 106-109.

[24] Source: Veronika Oleksyn, "Horse dreams dashed, German teen turns to cow Luna." Associated Press. 5 April 2011 <http://www.seattlepi.com/news/article/Horse-dreams-dashed-German-teen-turns-to-cow-Luna-1322827.php>.

[25] Source: Eric Carle, *Flora and Tiger: 19 Very Short Stories from My Life*, pp. 30-31, 38-39.

[26] Source: Eric Carle, *Flora and Tiger: 19 Very Short Stories from My Life*, pp. 50-51.

[27] Source: Peter C. Jones and Lisa MacDonald *Hero Dogs: 100 True Stories of Daring Deeds*, pp. 92-93.

[28] Source: Connie Schultz, "Honor Thy Children, Too." Creators Syndicate) 27 April 2011 <http://www.creators.com/liberal/connie-schultz/honor-thy-children-too-11-04-27.html>.

[29] Source: Logan Munger Brady, *Amusing Anecdotes*, p. 73.

[30] Source: Michèle Brown and Ann O'Connor, *Hammer and Tongues*, pp. 167-168.

[31] Source: Wendie C. Old, *Duke Ellington: Giant of Jazz*, pp. 105-107.

[32] Source: Bill Adler, *Jewish Wit and Wisdom*, p. 38.

[33] Source: Alicia Markova, *Markova Remembers*, pp. 11-13.

[34] Source: MarkGrace, post on "The 'Kids Say the Darndest Things' thread." Cougaruteforum.com. <http://cougaruteforum.com/showthread.php?t=16907>. Accessed on 15 April 2011. Also: Posts by "Clackamascoug" and "BigPiney" and "Cowboy."

[35] Source: *Anecdotes of the Hour By Famous Men*, pp. 50-51.

[36] Source: Wally, Post on "The 'Kids Say the Darndest Things' thread." Cougaruteforum.com. http://cougaruteforum.com/showthread.php?t=16907&page=2. Accessed on 14 April 2011.

[37] Source: JuneBug, "The Simple Kindness of a Four Year Old." Helpothers.org. 27 January 2011 <http://www.helpothers.org/story.php?sid=24624>.

[38] Source: Grace Fox, *Everyday Etiquette*, pp. 230-231.

[39] Source: Leo Slezak, *Song of Motley*, pp. 128-129.

[40] Source: Colleen Kenefick and Amy Y. Young, compilers and editors, *The Best of Nursing Humor*, p. 155.

[41] Source: George Zoritch, *Ballet Mystique: Behind the Glamour of the Ballet Russe*, p. 207.

[42] Source: Maria Sudekum Fisher, "Secret Santa Reveals His Identity." Associated Press. 18 November 2006 <http://www.facebook.com/topic.php?uid=2217761432&topic=1859>. Posted on Facebook. Also: Maria Sudekum Fisher, "Kansas City's Secret Santa dies." Associated Press. 13 January 2009 <http://www2.ljworld.com/news/2007/jan/13/kansas_citys_secret_santa_dies/>. Also: Maria Sudekum Fisher, "Kansas City's new Secret Santa keeps tradition of anonymous gifts going." Associated Press. 15 December 2009 <http://www.dallasnews.com/news/nation-world/nation/20091215-Kansas-City-s-new-Secret-Santa-3617.ece>.

[43] Source: Eugene R. Gryniewicz, "From Eugene R. Gryniewicz." *Random Acts of Kindness Stories.* Peopleandpossibilities.com. <http://www.peopleandpossibilities.com/33kindnessstories2.html>. Accessed 26 April 2011.

[44] Source: Anwahs, "Trespassing Snowmen." Dailygood.org. 26 December 2007 <http://www.dailygood.org/view.php?qid=4259>.

[45] Source: Lisa Bendall, "Santa Moonlighting as a Displaced Texan?." Wordpress.cpm. 18 December 2010 < http://50gooddeeds.wordpress.com/category/guest-stories/>.

[46] Source: Nat Hentoff, "The Duke, Before My Time." *Wall Street Journal.* 8 March 2011 <http://online.wsj.com/article/ SB10001424052748703791904576076282468283342.html?mod=WSJ_LifeStyle_Lifest

[47] Source: Bob Hope, *The Road to Hollywood*, pp. 38-40.

[48] Source: J. Bryan III, *Merry Gentlemen (and One Lady)*, p. 131.

[49] Source: Humphrey Procter-Gregg, *Beecham Remembered*, pp. 34-35.

[50] Source: Charles O'Connell, *The Other Side of the Record*, pp. 98-99.

[51] Source: Stanley Holloway, *Wiv a Little Bit O' Luck*, p. 195.

[52] Source: Margaret F. Atkinson and May Hillman, *Dancers of the Ballet*, p. 114.

[53] Source: Barbara Newman and Leslie E. Spatt, *Swan Lake*, p. 143.

[54] Source: Alan Wagner, *Prima Donnas and Other Wild Beasts*, p. 130.

[55] Source: Maxine Marx, *Growing Up with Chico*, p. 137.

[56] Source: Alexander Bland, *Fonteyn and Nureyev*, pp. 23, 52.

[57] Source: Rusty E. Frank, *Tap!*, pp. 88, 90, 92.

[58] Source: Anton Dolin, *Alicia Markova: Her Life and Art*, pp. 67-69. 81.

[59] Source: A.H. Franks, editor, *Pavlova: A Collection of Memoirs*, pp. 27, 90.

[60] Source: Robert Greskovic, *Ballet 101*, pp. 384, 392.

[61] Source: Alice Patelson, *Portrait of a Dancer, Memories of Balanchine*, pp. 22-23.

[62] Source: Suzanne Farrell, *Holding On to the Air*, pp. 79-80.

[63] Source: John Gruen, *People Who Dance*, p. 96.

[64] Source: Alice Patelson, *Portrait of a Dancer, Memories of Balanchine*, pp. 23-24.

[65] Source: Agnes de Mille, *Portrait Gallery*, p. 20.

[66] Source: Anton Dolin, *Alicia Markova: Her Life and Art*, p. 274.

[67] Source: Jim Haskins and N.R. Mitgang, *Mr. Bojangles*, p. 191.

[68] Source: John Gruen, *People Who Dance*, p. 46.

[69] Source: Theodore Stier, *With Pavlova Around the World*, pp. 57-59.

[70] Source: Alexander Bland, *Fonteyn and Nureyev*, p. 12.

[71] Source: "A child's death gives life to seven others." CNN. 24 May 1999 Posted on Dailygood.org. <http://www.dailygood.org/more.php?n=2461>.

[72] Source: Danny Thomas, *Make Room for Danny*, pp. 293-296.

[73] Source: Roger Ebert, Review of *Shoah*, A Great Movie. Posted 29 December 2010   <http://rogerebert.suntimes.com/apps/pbcs.dll/article?AID=/20101229/REVIEWS08/101229981>.

[74] Source: Groucho Marx, *The Secret Word is Groucho*, pp. 24, 132.

[75]   Source: Andrew Tobias, "Gold." 8 February 2011 <http://www.andrewtobias.com/newcolumns/110208.html>.

[76] Source: George Jessel, *Jessel, Anyone?*, p. 22.

[77] Source: John Burke, *Rogue's Progress: The Fabulous Adventures of Wilson Mizner*, pp. 67-68.

[78] Source: Ritch Shydner and Mark Schiff, compilers. *I Killed: True Stories of the Road from America's Top Comics*, p. 159.

[79] Source: Natalia Makarova, *A Dance Autobiography*, p. 50.

[80] Source: Willie Nelson, *The Facts of Life and Other Dirty Jokes*, pp. 63-64.

[81] Source: Ben Primack, adapter and editor, *The Ben Hecht Show*, p. 184.

[82] Source: Danny Thomas, *Make Room for Danny*, p. 303.

[83] Source: Merlin Holland, *The Wilde Album*, p. 128.

[84] Source: Frederick S. Voss, *Women of Our Time: An Album of Twentieth-Century Portraits*, pp. 150-151.

[85] Source: J. Bryan III, *Merry Gentlemen (and One Lady)*, p. 160.

[86] Source: Grace Fox, *Everyday Etiquette*, p. 191.

[87] Source: Nick Harris, *I Wish I'd Said That!*, p. 35.

[88] Source: George Sullivan, *Trapped*, pp. 34-53.

[89]   Source: Sister Helen P. Mrosla, "All the Good Things." Crystal-reflections.com   <http://www.crystal-reflections.com/stories/story_15.htm>. Accessed on 24 April 2010. Also: "All the Good Things." Snopes. <http://www.snopes.com/glurge/allgood.asp>. Accessed on 24 April 2010. Also: Chelsea J. Carter, "I Have to Praise You Like I Should." Associated Press. 6 February 1999. Posted at http://goodnewschannel.blogspot.com/2005_12_01_archive.html.

[90] Source: Jay Alabaster, "Tsunami-hit towns forgot warnings from ancestors." Associated Press. 6 April 2011 <http://www.star-telegram.com/2011/04/06/2979300/tsunami-hit-towns-forgot-warnings.html>.

[91] Source: "Tsunami hero girl sees U.N., meets Clinton." *U.S. Water News Online.* November 2005 <http://www.uswaternews.com/archives/arcglobal/5tsunhero11.html>.

[92]Source: Joe Hyams, *Zen in the Martial Arts*, pp. 35-36.

[93] Source: "Is your living in vain?" Crystal-reflections.com. <http://www.crystal-reflections.com/stories/story_103.htm>. Accessed on 9 April 2011.

[94] Source: Leonard S. Marcus, compiler and editor, *Funny Business: Conversations with Writers of Comedy*, p. 72.

[95]Source: Carmen Bredeson, *Ruth Bader Ginsburg: Supreme Court Justice*, pp. 57-58.

[96]Source: Logan Munger Brady, *Amusing Anecdotes*, p. 141.

[97]Source: Illaria Obidenna Ladré, *Illaria Obidenna Ladré: Memoirs of a Child of Theatre Street*, p. 9.

[98] Source: Leonard S. Marcus, compiler and editor, *Funny Business: Conversations with Writers of Comedy*, p. 191.

[99]Source: Nicolas Legat, *Ballet Russe*, p. 22.

[100] Source: Kevyn Aucoin, *The Art of Makeup*, pp. 40-141.

[101]Source: Leo Rosten, *People I Have Loved, Known or Admired*, p. 227.

[102]Source: Russell Johnson and Steve Cox, *Here on Gilligan's Isle*, p. 173.

[103] Source: Roger Ebert, "My old man." Roger Ebert's Journal. 18 March 2010 <http://blogs.suntimes.com/ebert/2010/03/my_old_man.html>.

[104] Source: Marlo Thomas, *Growing Up Laughing: My Story and the Story of Funny*, pp. 23-26.

[105] Source: Jennifer Wolcott, "Lunch lady with a mission: getting kids to eat healthy." *The Christian Science Monitor.* 21 March 2007 <http://www.csmonitor.com/2007/0321/p13s02-legn.html>.

[106] Source: Trisha Yearwood, *Georgia Cooking in an Oklahoma Kitchen*, pp. 42, 112.

[107] Source: Frederick E. Maser and Robert Drew Simpson, *If Saddlebags Could Talk*, p. 66.

[108]Source: Alexandra Danilova, *Choura*, p. 152.

[109]Source: Alexandra Danilova, *Choura*, p. 84.

[110] Source: Molly Ringwald, *Getting the Pretty Back: Friendship, Family, and Finding the Perfect Lipstick*, p. 196.

[111]Source: James Klosty, editor and photographer, *Merce Cunningham*, p. 58.

[112]Source: Nathaniel Benchley, *Robert Benchley*, p. 213.

[113]Source: Ted Shawn, *One Thousand and One Night Stands*, p. 169.

[114]Source: Corey Ford, *The Time of Laughter*, p. 98.

[115]Source: Tim Boxer, *The Jewish Celebrity Hall of Fame*, p. 252.

[116]Source: Tim Boxer, *The Jewish Celebrity Hall of Fame*, p. 267.

[117] Source: Debbie Anderson, "From His wife, Debbie Anderson." People and possibilities.com. <http://www.peopleandpossibilities.com/33kindnessstories2.html>. Accessed 21 April 2011.

[118] Source: Molly Ringwald, *Getting the Pretty Back: Friendship, Family, and Finding the Perfect Lipstick*, p. 87.

[119] Source: Jacqueline L. Salmon, "Professor Finds Fulfillment In Emptying His Pockets: D.C. Man's Charity Nearing $770,000." *Washington Post*. 11 June 2005 <http://www.washingtonpost.com/wp-dyn/content/article/2005/06/10/AR2005061001843.html>.

[120] Source: Donita Naylor, "Acts of kindness meet their interior design plan." *Providence Journal* (Rhode Island). 29 April 2010 <http://www.projo.com/news/content/DESIGN_IT_FORWARD_04-29-10_F2I9J8G_v11.39fbfa7.html>. Also: "Pay It Forward. <http://www.catherineryanhyde.com/pay-it-forward/>. Accessed on 26 February 20100.

[121] Source: Owen Hearey, "Humble grocer quietly gave away millions: Waldemar Kaminski's death unlocks his story." *Buffalo (New York) News*. 23 June 2006 <http://www.forgottenbuffalo.com/buffalospoloniahistory/kaminskimeats.html>.

[122] Source: Rob Young, "Single mother's wallet, $2,100 returned." *Appeal-Democrat*. 23 February 2011 <http://www.appeal-democrat.com/articles/single-104320-mother-children.html>.

[123] Source: Mitchell, "A Teenage Boy 'Starts at the Heart.'" Helpothers.org. 1 March 2011 <http://www.helpothers.org/story.php?sid=25060>.

[124] Source: Tyrone Curry, "Millionaire Janitor Buys School New Track." KING5. 19 April 2011 <http://www.msnbc.msn.com/id/42651800/ns/us_news-giving/>.

[125] Source: Peter C. Jones and Lisa MacDonald *Hero Dogs: 100 True Stories of Daring Deeds*, pp. 84-85.

[126] Source: Susanna Baird, "Fifth-Grade Crossing Guards Pull Small Students to Safety." AOL News. 14 April 2011 <http://www.aolnews.com/2011/04/14/fifth-grade-crossing-guards-pull-small-students-to-safety/>. Also: "Fifth-Grade Boy Getting Award For Saving Girl: 'I Just Wanted To Keep Her Safe,' Boy Says." KPTV.com. 13 April 2011 <http://www.kptv.com/education/27530862/detail.html>.

[127] Source: Barbara Liston, "British Tourist Saves Baby in 4-Story Florida Fall." Reuters. 21 April 2011 <http://www.msnbc.msn.com/id/42710443/ns/us_news-wonderful_world/>. Also: Barbara Liston, "British tourist who caught falling baby: I'm no hero." Reuters. 22 April 2011 <http://www.msnbc.msn.com/id/42724462/ns/us_news-wonderful_world/>.

[128] Source: Susanna Baird, "San Quentin Inmates Rescue Boaters From Bay." AOLnews.com. 21 April 2011 <http://www.aolnews.com/2011/04/21/san-quentin-inmates-rescue-boaters-from-bay/>.

[129] Source: Steve Cofield, "Hours before the biggest fight of his life, Jones subdues a robber." 19 March 2011 <http://sports.yahoo.com/mma/blog/cagewriter/post/Hours-before-biggest-fight-of-his-life-Jones-an;_ylt=Ajjd6Vt2aG5oDLNiZ5SFkUE9Eo14?urn=mma-wp309>.

[130] Source: "Kids, Ages 12 And 10, Chase Mother's Purse Snatcher." WFTV.com. 29 March 2011 <http://www.wftv.com/news/27356389/detail.html>. Also: "Two Children Chase Down Purse Thief." WFTV.com. 29 March 2011 <http://www.wftv.com/news/27351867/detail.html>.

[131] Source: Zora von Burden, editor, *Women of the Underground: Music*, pp. 137-138.

[132] Source: Darryl Lyman, *The Jewish Comedy Catalog*, p. 228.

[133] Source: Art Linkletter, *Women are My Favorite People*, p. 42.

[134] Source: Lewis C. Henry, *Humorous Anecdotes About Famous People*, p. 131.

[135] Source: Albert E. Kahn, *Days With Ulanova*, p. 96.

[136] Source: Michèle Brown and Ann O'Connor, *Hammer and Tongues*, p. 55.

[137] Source: Art Linkletter, *Women are My Favorite People*, p. 28.

[138] Source: Wendy Neale, *Ballet Life Behind the Scenes*, p. 150.

[139] Source: Barbara Woollcott, *None But a Mule*, pp. 88-89.

[140] Source: Corey Ford, *The Time of Laughter*, p. 68.

[141] Source: Richard Fountain, compiler, *The Wit of the Wig*, p. 10.

[142] Source: Tom Mullen, *Living Longer and Other Sobering Possibilities*, pp. 5, 11.

[143] Source: Lewis C. Henry, *Humorous Anecdotes About Famous People*, pp. 55-56.

[144] Source: Nick Harris, *I Wish I'd Said That!*, p. 104.

[145] Source: Maxine Marx, *Growing Up with Chico*, pp. 97-98, 166-168.

[146] Source: Richard Fountain, compiler, *The Wit of the Wig*, pp. 89-90.

[147] Source: Davida Kristy, *George Balanchine: American Ballet Master*, pp. 59-60.

[148] Source: Wanda Rutkowska, *Famous People in Anecdotes*, p. 11.

[149] Source: Ben Primack, adapter and editor, *The Ben Hecht Show*, p. 211.

[150] Source: John J. McPhaul, *Deadlines and Monkeyshines: The Fabled World of Chicago Journalism*, p. 135.

[151] Source: Kevyn Aucoin, *The Art of Makeup*, p. 18.

[152] Source: John J. McPhaul, *Deadlines and Monkeyshines: The Fabled World of Chicago Journalism*, pp. 123-124.

[153] Source: Wendy Neale, *Ballet Life Behind the Scenes*, pp. 96-97.

[154] Source: Stephen Schochet, *Hollywood Stories: Short, Entertaining Anecdotes About the Stars and Legends of the Movies!*, p. 35.

[155] Source: Sarah Montague, *Pas de Deux*, p. 25.

[156] Source: Jack and Waltraud Karkar, compilers and editors, ... *And They Danced On*, p. 28.

[157]Source: George Zoritch, *Ballet Mystique: Behind the Glamour of the Ballet Russe*, p. 119.

[158]Source: Hugh Vickers, *Even Greater Operatic Disasters*, p. 74.

[159]Source: Jan Greenberg and Sandra Jordan, *Andy Warhol: Prince of Pop*, p. 22.

[160]Source: Sarah Montague, *Pas de Deux*, p. 43.

[161] Source: Craig Marberry, *Cuttin' Up: Wit and Wisdom from Black Barber Shops*, p. 136.

[162]Source: Natalia Makarova, *A Dance Autobiography*, p. 48.

[163]Source: Alicia Markova, *Giselle and Me*, p. 183.

[164]Source: Walter Terry, *Ted Shawn: Father of American Dance*, p. 51.

[165]Source: Anna Russell, *I'm Not Making This Up, You Know*, p. 167.

[166]Source: Hugh Vickers, *Even Greater Operatic Disasters*, p. 41.

[167]Source: Joyce Grenfell, *Joyce Grenfell Requests the Pleasure*, p. 128.

[168] Source: Andrew Tobias, "Charles' Relationship to Money." Daily Column. 25 February 2011 <http://www.andrewtobias.com/newcolumns/110225.html >.

[169] Source: Stephen Schochet, *Hollywood Stories: Short, Entertaining Anecdotes About the Stars and Legends of the Movies!*, pp. 68-69.

[170]Source: Alicia Markova, *Markova Remembers*, p. 32.

[171]Source: John Burke, *Rogue's Progress: The Fabulous Adventures of Wilson Mizner*, p. 200.

[172]Source: Jan Greenberg and Sandra Jordan, *Andy Warhol: Prince of Pop*, pp. 41-42.

[173]Source: John Gregory, editor, *Heritage of a Ballet Master*, pp. 23, 25.

[174]Source: Davida Kristy, *George Balanchine: American Ballet Master*, p. 78.

[175]Source: Wanda Rutkowska, *Famous People in Anecdotes*, p. 6.

[176] Source: Zora von Burden, editor, *Women of the Underground: Music*, pp. 181, 187.

[177]Source: Humphrey Procter-Gregg, *Beecham Remembered*, pp. 157-158.

[178]Source: Hal Drucker and Sid Lerner, *From the Desk Of*, p. 64.

[179]Source: Joyce Grenfell, *Joyce Grenfell Requests the Pleasure*, pp. 159-160.

[180]Source: Charles O'Connell, *The Other Side of the Record*, p. 98.

[181]Source: Wendie C. Old, *Louis Armstrong: King of Jazz*, p. 67.

[182] Source: Chip Deffaw, *Jazz Veterans: A Portrait Gallery*, p. 24.

[183] Source: David Blum, *Quintet: Five Journeys Toward Musical Fulfillment*, p. 142.

[184] Source: Scott Beach, *Musicdotes*, p. 78.

[185] Source: Robert Greskovic, *Ballet 101*, pp. 41, 111, 117-118, 163, 193, 315.

[186] Source: H. Algeranoff, *My Years With Pavlova*, p. 141.

[187] Source: David Blum, *Quintet: Five Journeys Toward Musical Fulfillment*, p. 157. Also: John Gregory, editor, *Heritage of a Ballet Master*, p. 31.

[188] Source: John Javna, *The Best of TV Sitcoms*, p. 12.

[189] Source: Agnes de Mille, *Portrait Gallery*, pp. 108-109.

[190] Source: Ted Shawn, *One Thousand and One Night Stands*, p. 35.

[191] Source: Nathaniel Benchley, *Robert Benchley*, p. 214.

[192] Source: Leo Rosten, *People I Have Loved, Known or Admired*, p. 88.

[193] Source: Russell Johnson and Steve Cox, *Here on Gilligan's Isle*, pp. xviii-xix. Also: "Foreword," by Sherwood Schwartz, in Russell Johnson and Steve Cox's *Here on Gilligan's Isle*, p. xiii.

[194] Source: Gyles Brandreth, *Great Theatrical Disasters*, p. 72.

[195] Source: Hesketh Pearson, *Lives of the Wits*, p. 193.

[196] Source: Jack and Waltraud Karkar, compilers and editors, ... *And They Danced On*, p. 119.

[197] Source: Frederick E. Maser and Robert Drew Simpson, *If Saddlebags Could Talk*, p. 58.

[198] Source: Alicia Markova, *Markova Remembers*, pp. 110-111.

[199] Source: Bob Denver, *Gilligan, Maynard and Me*, p. 30.

[200] Source: Jim Haskins and N.R. Mitgang, *Mr. Bojangles*, pp. 218-219.

[201] Source: Wendie C. Old, *Duke Ellington: Giant of Jazz*, p. 73-74.

[202] Source: S. Hurok, *S. Hurok Presents*, p. 61.

[203] Source: Martha McNey, *Leslie's Story*, pp. 6, 14, 17.

[204] Source: Anna Russell, *I'm Not Making This Up, You Know*, pp. 115-116.

[205] Source: Joe Hyams, *Zen in the Martial Arts*, pp. 26-27.

[206] Source: Post by Mike Desert. Bikini Kill Archive. <http://bikinikillarchive.wordpress.com/>. Accessed on 11 March 2011.

[207]Source: Sir Rudolf Bing, *5000 Nights at the Opera*, p. 191.

[208]Source: Walter Terry, *Ted Shawn: Father of American Dance*, p. 152.

[209]Source: Wendie C. Old, *Louis Armstrong: King of Jazz*, pp. 90, 92.

[210]Source: S. Hurok, *S. Hurok Presents*, p. 115.

[211]Source: James Klosty, editor and photographer, *Merce Cunningham*, p. 76.

[212]Source: Alan Wagner, *Prima Donnas and Other Wild Beasts*, p. 99

[213]Source: Nicolas Legat, *Ballet Russe*, p. 28.

[214]Source: Margot Fonteyn, *Autobiography*, p. 150.

[215]Source: Margaret F. Atkinson and May Hillman, *Dancers of the Ballet*, pp. 90-91.

[216]Source: Ben Hecht, *Charlie: The Improbable Life and Times of Charles MacArthur*, p, 133.

[217]Source: Margot Fonteyn, *Autobiography*, pp. 92, 151.

[218] Source: *Anecdotes of the Hour By Famous Men*, p. 128.

[219]Source: Roxane Orgill, *Shout, Sister, Shout!*, p. 86.

[220]Source: Theodore Stier, *With Pavlova Around the World*, pp. 146-147.

[221] Source: Chip Deffaw, *Jazz Veterans: A Portrait Gallery*, p. 229.

[222] Source: Guerilla Girls, *Bitches, Bimbos and Ballbreakers: The Guerilla Girls' Illustrated Guide to Female Stereotypes*, p. 15.

[223]Source: Martha McNey, *Leslie's Story*, p. 12, 14, 21-22.

[224]Source: H. Algeranoff, *My Years With Pavlova*, pp. 117, 136.

[225]Source: A.H. Franks, editor, *Pavlova: A Collection of Memoirs*, pp. 91, 101.

[226] Source: Frederick S. Voss, *Women of Our Time: An Album of Twentieth-Century Portraits*, pp. 34-35.

[227]Source: Illaria Obidenna Ladré, *Illaria Obidenna Ladré: Memoirs of a Child of Theatre Street*, p. 37.

[228]Source: Gordon Irving, compiler, *The Wit of the Scots*, p. 22.

[229]Source: Bill Adler, *Jewish Wit and Wisdom*, p. 15.

[230]Source: Peg Bracken, *But I Wouldn't Have Missed It for the World!*, p. 46.

[231] Source: Heather Knight, "911 dispatcher honored for helping homeless." *San Francisco Chronicle*. 14 February 2008 <http://articles.sfgate.com/2008-02-14/bay-area/17141591_1_hats-gloves-packets>.

[232] Source: Guerilla Girls, *Bitches, Bimbos and Ballbreakers: The Guerilla Girls' Illustrated Guide to Female Stereotypes*, p. 50.

[233] Source: Ben Hecht, *Charlie: The Improbable Life and Times of Charles MacArthur*, p. 19.

[234] Source: Rosalyn M. Story, *And So I Sing: African-American Divas of Opera and Concert*, p. 150.

[235] Source: John Javna, *The Best of TV Sitcoms*, p. 84.

[236] Source: Jack Goodman and Albert Rice, *I Wish I'd Said That!*, p. 55.

[237] Source: Bob Denver, *Gilligan, Maynard and Me*, p. 160.

[238] Source: Sarah Giles, *Fred Astaire: His Friends Talk*, pp. 34, 139.

[239] Source: Jack Goodman and Albert Rice, *I Wish I'd Said That!*, pp. 79-80.

[240] Source: Scott Beach, *Musicdotes*, p. 67.

[241] Source: Sarah Giles, *Fred Astaire: His Friends Talk*, pp. 3, 26.

[242] Source: Yoel Rappel, *Yearning for the Holy Land: Hasidic Tales of Israel*, pp. 157-158.

[243] Source: Sir Rudolf Bing, *5000 Nights at the Opera*, p. 63.

[244] Source: Rusty E. Frank, *Tap!*, pp. 83, 85.

[245] Source: Albert E. Kahn, *Days With Ulanova*, p. 174.

[246] Source: Willie Nelson, *The Facts of Life and Other Dirty Jokes*, pp. 25, 27.

[247] Source: Merlin Holland, *The Wilde Album*, pp. 122, 125.

[248] Source: Barbara Newman and Leslie E. Spatt, *Swan Lake*, p. 39.

[249] Source: Suzanne Farrell, *Holding On to the Air*, p. 247.

[250] Source: Hesketh Pearson, *Lives of the Wits*, p. 180.